Think
Strategically

Think
Strategically

Plan the future and make it happen

ANDY BRUCE
KEN LANGDON

**LONDON, NEW YORK,
MUNICH, MELBOURNE, and DELHI**

Produced for Dorling Kindersley
by **terry jeavons**&**company**

Project Editor	Fiona Biggs
Project Art Editor	Terry Jeavons
Designer	J. C. Lanaway
Special Photography	Mike Hemsley

Senior Editor	Simon Tuite
Editor	Tom Broder
US Editor	Margaret Parrish
Senior Art Editor	Sara Robin
DTP Designer	Traci Salter
Production Controller	Stuart Masheter
Executive Managing Editor	Adèle Hayward
Managing Art Editor	Nick Harris
Art Director	Peter Luff
Publisher	Stephanie Jackson

First American Edition, 2007

Published in the United States by DK Publishing,
375 Hudson Street, New York, New York 10014

07 08 09 10 11 10 9 8 7 6 5 4 3 2 1

ED253—September 2007

Published in the United Kingdom by Dorling
Kindersley Ltd.

A catalog record for this book is available from
the Library of Congress

ISBN: 978-0-7566-3174-1

DK books are available at special discounts when
purchased in bulk for sales promotions, premiums,
fund-raising, or educational use. For details, contact:
DK Publishing Special Markets, 375 Hudson
Street, New York, New York 10014 or
SpecialSales@dk.com.

Printed and bound in China by Leo Paper Group
Discover more at www.dk.com

Contents

1 Prepare to Think Strategically

2 Analyze Your Situation

Introduction

No organization can succeed without effective strategic thinking; indeed, human beings cannot thrive and enjoy life if they do not think about the future for themselves, for their team, for their organization, and for their families and friends. Strategic thinking is, therefore, a key competency for anyone working in an organization.

Strategic thinkers have agreed on a plan for the future. They know how to translate their vision into a practical strategic plan that they can implement and improve as things around them change. They understand the planning process, how to motivate those with an interest in the plan (their stakeholders) to take part in the planning process, and accept responsibility for implementing the strategy. So, whether you are a chief executive or a member of a team striving to perform to its real potential, you will need to develop the skills that will improve performance.

> **Every successful plan has a good strategy behind it**

Think Strategically helps you to assess your current skills in this area and then guides you through every aspect of the thinking and planning process. It takes you from defining

your purpose and understanding
your unique contribution to
choosing the strategic emphasis
of the plan now and into the
future. It shows you how to plan
simple and complex changes your
team will need to make when
adapting to new circumstances,

by defining and implementing change projects.
It also looks at your work/life balance and other aspects
of your personal strategy, showing you how to play an
important part in the success of your organization while
meeting your personal goals.

If you find that you spend too much time firefighting,
unable to address the fundamental problems at work
because you are too busy dealing with the symptoms, you
will find a step-by-step guide to breaking out of this vicious
cycle. If work is swamping your life so that you are living to
work rather than working to live, you will discover how
to achieve a balance where your performance at work hits
new highs, your career soars, and you still have time for the
other important people in your life—and for some fun, too!

Assessing Your Skills

This questionnaire will get you to think about your strategic thinking skills and assess your scope for improvement. Complete it before reading the book, writing the appropriate letter in the "Before" box. After you have read the book, complete the questionnaire a second time to assess your progress.

Before **After**

1 Does your team plan fit in with your organization's strategy?

A I am not sure what my organization's strategy is.
B I have to take a different line in some circumstances because of my particular job.
C I can link my plan directly to the vision and objectives of the organization.

2 How well do you understand your customers' requirements?

A They tell us what they need and then we try to catch up with them.
B We have regular reviews with them twice a year.
C My strategy includes a system to regularly assess their changing requirements.

3 How well do you understand your competition?

A My customer is internal so I don't have any competition.
B I keep an eye on what they are doing.
C I understand the competition well now and am looking to the future.

4 How innovative is your team?

A We are good at reacting to new situations.
B We have a suggestion box that I check regularly.
C I have a system for examining and assessing new ways of doing things.

5 **When do you decide that you need to change the way you work?**

- **A** When circumstances make it unavoidable.
- **B** We review our methods in a planning session that is held twice a year.
- **C** We check continuously to see how we need to change to preempt problems.

6 **Will your plan endure in the long term?**

- **A** It's impossible to predict the future.
- **B** I think so; but we can be flexible.
- **C** It's part of our planning process to look at future possibilities.

7 **Do you understand the best product/market segments you should be in?**

- **A** I'm not sure what you mean by product/market.
- **B** This is rather driven by the opportunities that present themselves.
- **C** Yes, and we have activities in place to change emphasis where necessary.

8 **Do your boss and other stakeholders understand your strategy?**

- **A** Frankly, they are not interested.
- **B** I make an annual presentation.
- **C** We have a communications plan that keeps everyone up to date.

9 **Do you look for outside contractors to take over work where that is effective and cost effective?**

- **A** Is that not a little like handing your job over to someone else?
- **B** We would do that only when a major department is outsourced.
- **C** When planning we never assume that there is no other way of operating, including outsourcing.

10 **How well do you know how each change project fits in with others?**

- **A** We do not have change projects.
- **B** We tend to discover resource clashes and put them right before they become a problem.
- **C** We have a matrix of all the change projects, showing how they complement each other so that we can avoid duplication and learn from each other.

	Before	After

11 Has your risk assessment shown itself to be accurate?

- **A** We have no system for risk assessment.
- **B** We take some time out to try to predict problems.
- **C** We have a system for measuring the impact and urgency of potential problems.

12 Do you review your operational targets frequently as your strategy changes?

- **A** Our targets are set for us once a year.
- **B** If something changes we can revise an operational target as we go.
- **C** We check to see that a change in strategy might increase an operational target.

13 How well do you motivate your people to accept and take part in change?

- **A** If they have to change they have to change.
- **B** We find that change is usually accepted grudgingly over time.
- **C** We involve all stakeholders so that they get no surprises with a new strategy, we have a good reward system in place, and we make sure that people know they are appreciated.

14 Do you have a plan to achieve and maintain your work/life balance?

- **A** I have no choice at this stage.
- **B** I get home as often as possible.
- **C** I have agreed on the boundaries between work and life and strive to keep to them.

Final Scores

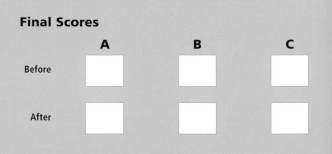

	A	B	C
Before			
After			

Analysis
Mostly As
Your answers suggest that you are fairly new to strategic thinking, and while you may be enthusiastic you need to think about the basic techniques of strategy setting and the planning process. Think first about your team's purpose and its unique contribution. Then work on the planning process to make sure that you understand each stage and are confident about how far you have gotten at any point in time. Think more about your customers and what their needs and wants are.

Mostly Bs
You have some knowledge of strategic thinking and deal with your stakeholders and customers fairly well. You are starting to see your strategy from the organization's point of view but you need to put more time and energy into improving your skills in this area. Start with a planning session and at least one change project and make a methodical plan. Be very self-critical of your overall approach to strategic thinking.

Mostly Cs
You certainly have a professional approach to your role as a team leader and strategic planner. Make sure, however, that you establish a good rapport with your customers and stakeholders as well as treating them professionally. Concentrate on the long-term strategy and use some of the techniques in this book to help you to improve the environment in which you work and your operational performance. Use these techniques to assist other people in your team to improve their skills. Show them how important it is to be in control of their work and their lives by reviewing and amending the strategy when necessary.

Conclusion
If this is the first time you have done this self-assessment, then keep in mind the analysis as you read the book. Pay special attention to the areas highlighted by your responses and take on board the tips and techniques—these will help you to reduce the number of A responses next time around, and will help you to achieve a more balanced mixture of Bs and Cs. After you have read the book and have had a chance to put the techniques into practice, take the quiz again. Provided you have answered honestly, you will be able to measure your progress and should see a big improvement.

Prepare to Think Strategically 1

It is vital to understand what strategy is and to recognize what you need to do to fit in with and contribute toward the strategy of your organization, assist in the production of your team strategy, and take your personal aspirations into account. This chapter will show you how to:

- Understand how an organizational strategy impacts your team and you as an individual
- Define the process of developing a strategic framework for a plan
- Recognize the importance of making time for strategic planning
- Work out your work/life balance

The Importance of Strategy

The ability to differentiate short- and long-term thinking and strike a balance between the two is an integral part of strategy. If you understand the role of each you will find it easier to achieve the right combination.

Set Personal Aspirations

The organization that you work for has a carefully planned strategy for the future. It knows where it wants to be in one year's time in detail, in three year's time in outline and in five year's time as a framework. Without that strategy it would not be able to maximize its potential. Think about yourself in terms of a personal strategy. Do you know where you want to be in three to five years time? Do you have a personal aspiration that covers the long term, not only in career terms but also as a whole work/life framework? Like your organization, you need a strategy to make sure you maximize your potential. You can use this framework to check that what you are doing in the short term helps you toward your long term goals and aspirations.

Think short and long term

A good strategy will strike a balance between short- and long-term thinking. If you focus entirely on short-term success you risk long-term failure. Suppose, for example, you are making good revenues and profits out of importing and selling analog radios and that it has been a successful product for some time. If you ignore the fact that there is going to be a switchover to digital radios over the next few years you will be trying and failing to sell products into a market that has moved on, but if you place undue emphasis on long-term planning, today's business will inevitably suffer simply because you will not have the resources or income to survive into the long term. The key is to focus on the present to achieve the personal and organizational growth you need now, and to keep one eye on the future to ensure that good decisions today are just as beneficial for your strategy tomorrow.

Create an Urgency and Impact Matrix

This matrix will help you to define the impact and urgency of each issue so that you can prioritize the most important tasks for your strategy.

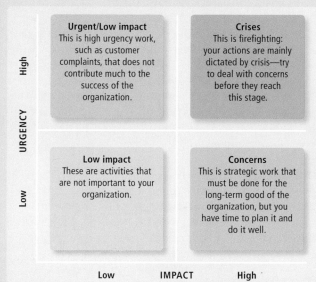

URGENCY

High

Urgent/Low impact
This is high urgency work, such as customer complaints, that does not contribute much to the success of the organization.

Crises
This is firefighting: your actions are mainly dictated by crisis—try to deal with concerns before they reach this stage.

Low

Low impact
These are activities that are not important to your organization.

Concerns
This is strategic work that must be done for the long-term good of the organization, but you have time to plan it and do it well.

Low   **IMPACT**   **High**

Plan to Succeed A well-planned strategy will help everyone to work more successfully and efficiently, not just those who work in the boardroom.

Understand the Levels of Strategy

Strategic plans consist of three levels—organizational, team, and personal plans. The strategic planning process is the method by which organizations, teams, and you as as an individual focus on maximizing performance.

How the Levels Work Together

Organizations operate in a changing world. Senior managers review and revise organizational strategy to take account of this change, then brief their operating units on the strategy and their role within it. This allows divisions, departments, and your team to plan their strategies within the organizational framework. Set your personal goals and objectives to make sure you meet your operational targets and have a personal development programme to suit your long-term aspirations.

Organizational Strategy

All organizations start reviewing their strategic plans by arriving at a thorough understanding of their current capabilities and business processes. They then search for a fit between these and the external business environment as they see it. This allows them to choose their way ahead, or their "mission." From this they can define their current and future products and services and the markets into which they will sell them. The organization looks specifically for its prime source or sources of advantage—the elements of its capabilities that set it apart from other organizations, particularly its competitors in the business. Everyone, not just senior managers, contributes to the overall organizational strategy. Team leaders should be the eyes and ears of the organization, identifying the need for strategic change that will enable the organization to move forward.

> The right plan will move any strategy in the right direction

Assessing a Company's Strategy

All organizations produce some sort of annual report outlining progress during the previous year and the organization's plans for the future. These reports can provide an insight into the strategy of the organization.

If you are hoping to learn something useful from an annual report, here are some things to look for:

→ **Mission statement**—Early on in the report you will see a short statement that illustrates what senior managers believe is the purpose of the organization.

→ **Financial highlights**—This is usually an indicator of where the organization's strategic emphasis lies.

→ **Chairman's statement**—This more or less encapsulates the strategic framework of the organization by stating what it is going to provide to which customers and how it will go about achieving this.

→ **Directors' reports**—These describe the structure of the organization and outline how the overall strategy percolates down to each level.

→ **Employee facts and figures**—The type and quality of the people in an organization is another key indicator of strategy.

Keep in Touch Discuss the company report to check that your team strategy is in line with the overall plans of the organization.

TIP To achieve optimum results, try breaking your work time into operational time, strategic thinking time, and professional development time.

Team Strategy

The team must deliver results in order to achieve specified objectives for the organizational strategy. The effectiveness of your team's strategy depends on a number of factors:

- **Involvement in the planning process**—Encourage your team to research facts, take part in creative team meetings, and brainstorm ideas and methods to identify the best possible way ahead. That way everyone is involved in setting the strategy and committed to carrying out the plan.
- **Accurate information**—At the start of the process, gather all the facts that will affect the team's strategy. Realistically, you will never have every item of data you need, but you should always strive to improve accuracy and avoid guesswork.

Work Together If you work with the members of your team to produce your strategic plan, they will be enthusiastic when it comes time to implement it.

- **Strong ideas**—Encourage people to come up with suggestions for improving the environment in which the team operates, from modifications to products or services to alterations to the business processes involved in performing the team's function. This improves the effectiveness with which the team can add innovative ideas into the planning process.
- **Commitment to the strategy**—Implementation of the plan demands extra effort by the team outside its normal operations, so gaining real commitment is vital.

If you get these four areas right you will be well on the way to producing a strategy that all the right people will agree with and commit to implementing.

Personal Strategy

You will have to work hard to achieve your team's goals, but make sure that you are fulfilling your personal aspirations as well. There are 168 hours in the week. Allowing for sleep, you have around 100 hours at your disposal. Make a list of your activities; such as friends, relationships, family, personal development, leisure, and work and figure out how many hours you spend on each. Now add new areas of activity you want to get involved in. Decide where you want to increase or decrease the number of hours. Try to implement these changes and you should fulfill your potential and enjoy life more.

The Strategic Planning Process

Analyze your external and internal environments

⬇

Create a strategic framework

⬇

Implement a strategic plan

⬇

Plan for the future

Focus on Strategy

It is easy for everyday pressures to distract you from your plans, but strategic planning is a continuous activity. Schedule time to prioritize strategic thinking and make sure that you keep your long-term goals in focus.

Prioritize Strategy

Ensure you make strategic planning a priority by deciding early in the project on the appropriate amount of time and resources you will need to dedicate to both operational and strategic thinking. For example, you might decide to set aside time in your calendar for three months in order to develop a new strategy, allocating two days of strategy meetings every week at the beginning of the project and then one day a week thereafter. This should leave you sufficient time to address operational issues adequately.

Plan Continually

Thinking and planning strategically is a continuous process. Even when you are implementing the results of your strategic thinking, it is important not to neglect future planning. Set aside time each month to discuss maintaining and developing the plan. The most successful business people allow at least half a day each week for the implementation of the strategic part of their jobs. Keep in mind that the more senior your job, the more time you should be spending on thinking strategically. It is your dedication to strategic planning that will ensure the long-term success of your organization.

You may need approval right away for a part of your strategic plan.

- Send an email that asks people to respond only if they are not in agreement. This is quicker than waiting for a positive response.

- Deal directly by telephone with people who contact you to express potential concerns.

Develop a Framework

Do not use the speed of change within your organization as an excuse for failing to plan or abandoning your strategy. Without a plan you will find that you are just reacting to everyday problems, rather than dealing with the underlying causes. Establish a framework to identify the strategic elements that you need to take into account whenever there is a significant change in your environment. Rather than

Plan to Succeed In order to implement your strategic plan you must keep your long-term objective in mind at all times and prevent yourself from being distracted by side issues.

changing your whole plan, you can attend to individual elements of the framework. You can also apply this strategic planning process in your personal life.

Keep Your Focus

Keep in mind at all times what your real objectives are. For example, if you are expecting a delivery of a printer with a page counter attachment and the supplier delivers one without that feature, think about what you really need to achieve before rejecting the delivery. Will a delay in delivery be more damaging than managing without the extra feature. If the printer that has been delivered meets all your key objectives you may be able to use the situation as a negotiating tool. Offer to keep the printer, but negotiate a discount to the price or some free print cartridges.

Summary: Thinking Strategically

The long-term future of your organization depends on innovative strategic thinking. Recognize its importance, make sure you understand how to define strategy, and work out an organizational, team, and personal strategy. If you are to be really effective you will have to try to get out of firefighting mode and take real control.

Taking Control

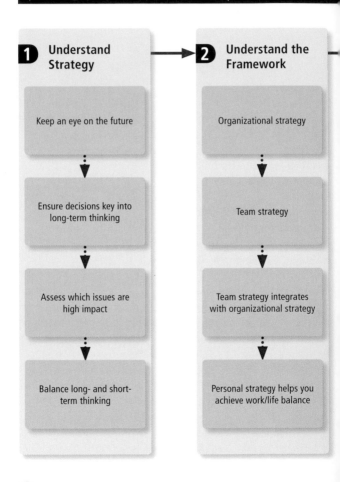

1 Understand Strategy

Keep an eye on the future

↓

Ensure decisions key into long-term thinking

↓

Assess which issues are high impact

↓

Balance long- and short-term thinking

2 Understand the Framework

Organizational strategy

↓

Team strategy

↓

Team strategy integrates with organizational strategy

↓

Personal strategy helps you achieve work/life balance

3 Focus on Strategy ➔ **4** Plan to Succeed

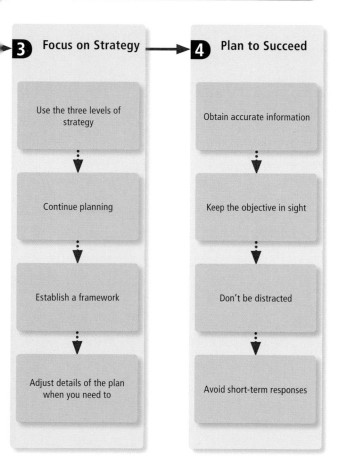

Use the three levels of strategy	Obtain accurate information
Continue planning	Keep the objective in sight
Establish a framework	Don't be distracted
Adjust details of the plan when you need to	Avoid short-term responses

Analyze Your Situation 2

A successful strategy depends to a great extent on the comprehensiveness and accuracy of the information that describes the situation that requires the strategy. This chapter shows you how to:

- Analyze and understand external and internal trends
- Understand your customers' present and future needs
- Discover your competitors' strengths and weaknesses
- Produce a summary of your skills and competencies in producing satisfied customers and fending off the competition

Analyze External Trends

A strategic framework will eventually lead to a series of change projects and actions. Start the process by studying trends to produce a thorough analysis of the impact of the external world on your strategy.

Assess the National and Global Economies

Ask yourself to what extent your organizational strategy depends on the economy in your own country or abroad. For example, if you are in the real estate business, you will be highly vulnerable to changes in interest rates. Make a list of the main economic trends that could affect your organization and find sources of information that will keep you up to date with these trends. You can use government statistics, of course, and the Internet is a good source of relevant information. If the data is highly significant, consider commissioning consultants' reports, which will address your situation specifically.

Look at Trends in Technology

There is one certainty that applies to almost any strategic plan: it will have to take into account the dramatic and ever-increasing changes that occur in technology. The importance of keeping up with these developments is paramount. Protect yourself from missing out on possible advances by discussing relevant technology matters at any planning meetings. Think about making one member of the team responsible for

5 minute FIX

If you need to gather information very quickly, limit the amount of data that you need to collect. Identify what you can get hold of easily and focus on that. For example, you could collect data on:

- The three economic trends that affect you the most

- The three main predictions with regard to technology that you already use

- Your biggest health and safety risk area

- Recent employment legislation.

keeping an eye on this. Give that person access to the reports of experts and analysts. Relevant and concise summaries of the information gleaned in this way can be passed on to the rest of the team.

Keep up with New Regulations

As an increasing number of organizations, particularly those operating in the public sector, find themselves working within regulatory frameworks, it is of paramount importance to understand exactly what the rules are. For example, if you are part of a government organization and there is a chance that a different political party will gain control during the life of your strategic plan you will have to take that into account so as not to make decisions that will have to be reversed in the near future. No matter what type of organization you work for, and in whatever sector it operates, you are subject to national and local employment laws and health and safety legislation. You may get all the relevant information from internal policy documents, or you may need to consult a lawyer who is an expert in the appropriate field. You should always make sure that any change in your strategy will not cause your organization to work outside the law. It is vital to pay attention to this area—mistakes can be costly and will give a poor impression of how your organization operates.

Make Information More Manageable

Make one member of your team responsible for looking at data

⬇

Give that person access to expert analysis

⬇

Pass on relevant information to the team

TIP Make information more manageable by looking at a piece of data and asking, "So what?" If the answer is "So nothing," disregard it and move on.

Understand Stakeholders' Needs

People with an interest in or an influence on a new strategy are known as "stakeholders." Foster good relationships—they can provide experience or information or can help with analysis or decision-making.

Listen to Stakeholders' Needs

Strategic planning often requires people from different parts of the organization to formulate a plan together. Involving the right people from the outset will greatly enhance your ability to agree on an effective strategy, gain commitment to it, and work within it. Consulting the right people at the right time will mean that there is less of a risk that your plan will become invalid because of a fundamental product change or a modification of your customers' needs. Such a spirit of cooperation produces the best results. The more involved people feel in the process the more likely they are to support and assist with the implementation of the strategic plan.

TECHNIQUES *to* practice

The key to working with stakeholders is to get quickly to their key issues, find out what they will agree to, and get them to commit to their role in the implementation. You can practice this in any stakeholder meeting by making sure that the minutes of the meeting record specifically the action that needs to be taken and the person who will be responsible for that action.

For example, when a stakeholder, such as the production manager, has suggested that it might be possible to change the strategy to use powder coating rather than putting gates through the paint shop, make sure that the minutes of the meeting record:

- Who is responsible for comparing the two possibilities
- Who this peson will need to talk to about it
- When she will report back to the stakeholder and the group.

Key Stakeholders and Their Roles

Stakeholder	Role
Your superior	Ensures that the new plan is consistent with other strategies in the organization
Expert	Provides specialized knowledge of problems or opportunities that might affect the plan
Backer	Supports the strategy by providing essential resources, such as people or budget, to assist in its implementation
Key customer/supplier	Provides valuable information on future requirements and new possibilities

Involve Your Team

An effective strategy depends upon an effective team, so you should involve it in the strategic planning process from the earliest stages. Many managers don't involve the team early on because they believe that not everyone will have a major involvement in implementing the strategy. Whole team planning is always useful in producing a more creative strategy. It gives team members the chance to decide if they are happy to work within the new strategy as it evolves or whether they feel they could make a bigger contribution in a different environment.

Assess Your Core Team

Involving key team members in strategic planning from the outset enables you to assess whether they have the qualities necessary to help you to bring the plan to fruition in the future. Your core team should include all those who will be responsible for implementing the plan and achieving its goals. If people feel involved in the project from the start they will work harder to achieve its objectives.

Junior team members often bring new insights to the plan

Find out What Customers Want

There are many useful techniques for establishing what your customers, both internal and external, want. Use a cross-section of these when planning to make sure that your strategy goes to the heart of their requirements.

Use Feedback

Direct feedback from customers helps you to understand their needs. Use multiple choice feedback forms, not only to help you to understand how satisfied your customers are at the moment but also to identify new trends so that your strategy can anticipate them. Make the questions very clear so that the replies you receive are completely unambiguous. When you have collated the feedback, use it to identify ways in which you can develop your strategy to meet customers' present needs and improve your service to them in the future.

TIP **View any customer meeting or contact as an opportunity to find out more about your customers.**

Know Your Customer
Make sure that you know exactly who your customer is—children have a big influence on the spending patterns of adults.

Set up Focus Groups

One of the most effective techniques for finding out what your customers really want is to bring a group of them together for a discussion that focuses on their concerns.

Get the right group together:

→ Make sure it is representative of your customers with regard to age, gender, and spending power.

→ You will need a group of between six and eight people to ensure a good range of views.

Get the atmosphere right:

→ Make the atmosphere very relaxed and unthreatening.

→ Encourage open and frank discussion.

→ Have someone from your team write comprehensive notes of what is said. Do not try to act as facilitator and minute taker.

Ask the right questions:

→ Use open questions. Ask, for example, "What is most important for you when deciding to buy?"

→ Other good openings include "Could you explain how...?"

Gather and maintain records of customer feedback so that you can refer to them when you are planning your strategy for introducing new products or entering new markets. Use this simple complaint record as a template:

Customer Feedback	
Date	02/03
Customer	Rohan Singh, The Bear Inn
Complaint	Error in bill repeated this month
Dealt with by	Constanza
Passed to	Richard
Report no.	Ccom09678

Identify Performance Criteria

Make sure that your customers are the main drivers of your strategy. Build customer loyalty by understanding the criteria they use when making a decision to buy or not to buy. Think of the questions they will ask when comparing your offering against alternatives or your competition. Speak to people in your organization or team who have direct contact with your customers, as well as talking to the customers themselves. Remember that prospective customers who have not yet decided to deal with you may have different criteria from your current customer base, so take them into account as well. Make a comprehensive list of these buying criteria when planning your strategy.

Customers' Buying Criteria

Area	Criteria	Customer ideal	Priority
Product	Quality	Zero faults	7
Product	Ease of use	No special training	10
Process	Ease of buying	Efficient order systems and fast delivery	8
Process	Administration	Accurate invoices and statements	6
People	Knowledge of their products and services	One person can answer all questions	3
People	Customer knowledge	Ability to relate products to customer needs	4
Price	Competitive	Lowest price	7
Price	Payment terms	Favorable credit terms to spread payments	6

If you have a close relationship with a customer you may need to step back to consider the bigger picture. The customer may hide concerns or changes in buying criteria in case it damages the relationship.

If you find that you can no longer assess a customer's priorities, ask someone who has had no direct dealings with your customer to fill in a matrix of buying criteria against the four main areas of product, process, people, and price, and to score each criterion according to the importance the customer has placed on that criterion in the past.

Establish the Ideal

Work out what your customers would like in an "ideal" world, so that you can gear yourself up to provide it. Ask yourself what they see as the ideal that a supplier could offer them in four areas—product, process, people, and price. Ask for their opinion, either in a meeting, on the telephone, or by inviting them to attend part of a planning session. The points conveyed in the information they give you are their buying criteria, and they will fit into one of the four main areas listed above. When you have established the criteria you can prioritize them. This will have a major impact on your plan.

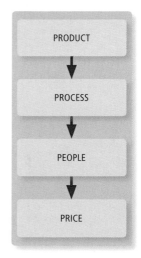

Use the Criteria Any change to the product, service, people, or price should always be made with reference to what your customers have indicated to you is important to them.

Analyze the Competition

You will satisfy your customers' needs only if you are better than the competition. Analyze your competitors' strengths and weaknesses so that you can take them into account when planning your strategy.

Examine Current Competition

Choose either your main competitor or a representative group of all your competitors for analysis. Obtain published material such as brochures and promotional materials to find out what they see as their competitive advantage. Check their website. Use third party information such as trade journals and reviews of products and services in newspapers and magazines for competitive comparisons. Do not forget that your own customers are also a good source of competitive information, as are new recruits to your organization from any competitor. Build up a picture of strengths and weaknesses by making

Always keep a sharp eye on the competition

Effective Ways to Analyze Competition

HIGH IMPACT

- Keeping an open mind about the shape of your strategy until you have finally completed the competition analysis stage
- Keeping control of discussions to prevent rash decisions
- Making a note of information about competitors
- Taking account of relevant third party information

NEGATIVE IMPACT

- Jumping from one piece of competitive information to inappropriate action
- Making competitive decisions in a mood of panic
- Only making notes about how you might react to any information about competitors
- Failing to consult trade journals and reviews for information

---

a chart of your competitor's ability to meet your customers' buying criteria. Establish how close the competition gets to the customer's ideal and, more importantly, identify where it is closer to the ideal than you are.

Anticipate Future Competition

Most organizations see their current competitors as providers of similar products or services. But this may not always be the case. Suppose you are a telephone service provider. Up until recently your competition has been confined to other telephone service providers using similar technology. However, your strategy now would have to take account of the fact that internet service providers can offer low-cost telephone calls using existing broadband connections. Always think about your customer's real objectives and requirements and guard against a new competitor offering an innovative solution. Don't fall into the trap of believing that because you supply the best product or service at the moment this will always be the case. Be alert to the danger of being outstripped by the competition—always remember that they are watching you constantly and learning from everything that you do.

Identify Competitive Opportunities and Threats

Make sure you translate competitive information into possible features of your strategy:

Identify where you are better able to meet your customers' priorities

⬇

Ask yourself, "How can we exploit this fact?"

⬇

Identify where your competitor is nearer to meeting your customers' ideal supplier criteria than you are

⬇

Think through what you could build into your strategy to reduce the threat

Understand Team Capabilities

Before deciding what will be your strategic way ahead, document the skills in your team and the processes it uses to provide customer satisfaction, and identify the competencies that you must always strive to improve.

Review Team Skills

Ask people to talk about their strengths and weaknesses in relation to meeting customer needs. Try to make them feel positive about the process. Remind them that they are, after all, formulating a new strategy that will bring the team greater success and more opportunities in the future. Review all resources as well as people; they should all be involved in some way with providing a service that delights the customer. Look at office accommodation and factory and warehouse space to assess how well they meet your needs now and how suitable they will be in the future. Similarly, look at machinery, vehicles, tools, and computer equipment, and establish whether any of these need to be replaced or upgraded to improve performance.

Talk about Strengths and Weaknesses

To overcome any nervousness that your people may experience in having a frank discussion about their skills, keep smiling and be positive. Start by discussing their strengths and thanking them for the contribution they have made to date. Use positive questions to identify areas where improvement may be necessary:

→ Can you suggest ways in which the whole team could improve its overall performance?

→ How has your job changed since you joined the organization and how do you see it changing in the future?

→ Do you recognize any training needs?

Examine Internal Business Processes

Examine your business processes using the two best sources of information—your customers and the people on your team who are involved in implementing the processes. You may need to review the way you take orders, revise terms and conditions—perhaps to meet a competitive threat—and reassess the after-sales service you provide. Look particularly for duplication, gaps, and frequent areas of complaint. Examine how well your information systems work. Ask members of the team to note instances when they have had to spend time chasing information that could have been contained in an accessible, regular report. Draw up a comprehensive list of gaps and decide which of these prevent the team offering a first-class service.

Find Clues to Problem Areas

When you look at your customer interface you will often detect clues about areas of your operation where improvements might be made. For example, if you always have to call customers back to respond to their questions because finding the answer takes a lot of time, you may need to address a problem with your system.

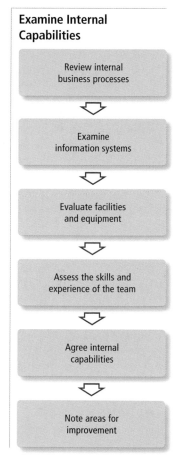

Examine Internal Capabilities

- Review internal business processes
- Examine information systems
- Evaluate facilities and equipment
- Assess the skills and experience of the team
- Agree internal capabilities
- Note areas for improvement

Identify Core Competencies

A core competency is an area of expertise; an area in which you specialize or offer something unique. Identify your core competencies and ensure that necessary skills are kept up to date. Consider outsourcing noncore tasks.

Outsource Noncore Activities

Your purpose is to focus on activities concerned with the delivery of your products and services to customers. Any other activity could be outsourced. Ask the question: "In order to be better than anyone else at what we do, what competencies and capabilities do we need?" For example, if your main product is software, you may decide never to use external software development resources, while outsourcing many other functions, such as:

- Facilities management to a serviced office provider
- Marketing to a company that specializes in finding sales leads
- Sales to several different channels.

The test on outsourcing is whether you can buy in any activities that can be done by others more efficiently and effectively without increasing the risk of delivering a poor service to your customers. Because core competencies are so important your team needs to be able to perform them better than anyone else can. Ask colleagues for recommendations before you decide to outsource any function—you will be putting your performance and reputation at risk.

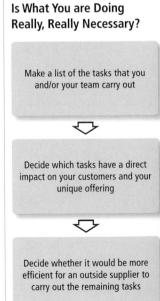

Is What You are Doing Really, Really Necessary?

Make a list of the tasks that you and/or your team carry out

⬇

Decide which tasks have a direct impact on your customers and your unique offering

⬇

Decide whether it would be more efficient for an outside supplier to carry out the remaining tasks

Case study: Stripping Down the Operation

Ron was the brand manager for a carbonated drinks company. In reviewing his strategy a year before he had identified his core competencies as managing and promoting the brand, making up the concentrated syrup for the drink, and manufacturing and bottling the product. While sales of the product had grown on target for the year, profits had not kept pace. When he was considering changes in strategy his manager, Betty, made him look at what his team did better than anyone else— brand management and production of the concentrate. This helped Ron to realize that manufacturing and bottling were not actually core competencies and he decided to outsource that operation.

- *By recognizing what his real core competencies were, Ron succeeded in stripping down his overheads and reducing the size of his team.*
- *He also managed to restore the all-important ratio between sales and profit growth.*

Stay Flexible

There is an argument that says you should determine your strategy by your existing skills. This is known as a capability driven strategy. It makes sense in that there is no point in developing a strategy that you are not in a position to implement. However, it carries the risk that there will be a poor fit between what you offer and what customers really want. Your competitors may be evolving into much more flexible organizations, able to buy in or develop new skills as they are required. This means that their current capabilities are much less of a

Flexibility will ensure the success of your strategy

barrier to changing strategy than they were in the past. Imagine what your strategy might be if you were to become similarly flexible and not limit, at this stage, what your eventual strategy might be.

Innovate Strategically

In most industries there is rapid change. Get into the habit of looking at new ideas, put in place a system to evaluate the ideas, and exploit them in sufficient time to continue to thrive as an organization.

Examine New Ideas

The formal planning process is the mechanism through which you will identify specific opportunities and threats. Looking for strategic innovation means contemplating different scenarios and possibilities for changes in how you operate. Look at the skills or information that you and your team create and maintain—is there any way in which you could use these in more effective or profitable ways?

Use Your Resources

For some years organizations have been buying other organizations for the sole purpose of gaining access to their customer databases. Establish whether your team could provide services to another part of your organization to improve its performance, or whether you could exploit the data to which you have access by selling it to a third party. Strategic innovation involves keeping one step ahead of your competitors by looking in this way at all the resources you control, at every product you manufacture, and at each market in which you operate. Keeping up to date in this way will give you a competitive edge.

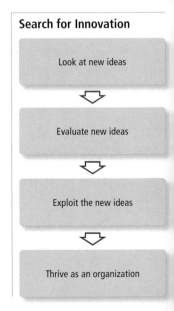

Search for Innovation

Look at new ideas

⇩

Evaluate new ideas

⇩

Exploit the new ideas

⇩

Thrive as an organization

Screen and Prioritize

Encourage people to come up with new ideas. Put in place a screening system that people can use to evaluate their own ideas. One of the most effective screening systems is "V-SAFE," which allows you to assess five criteria:

→ **Value**—What value will this add to the organization in terms of impact on organizational goals and objectives?
→ **Suitability**—Is this idea suitable given the current situation (and trends in the environment) and organization strategy?
→ **Acceptability**—Will all the key stakeholders necessary for implementation buy into this idea and actively support it?
→ **Feasibility**—Do we have the necessary resources in terms of people, facilities, equipment, materials, budget, and time?
→ **Endurance**—Will this idea provide enduring or long-term benefits in terms of continuing to meet organizational goals?

By making people aware of these criteria, they will start to self-screen ideas and think differently about their roles.

Having completed an initial screening, a formal business case can be developed for ideas that require significant investment. This will compare the financial benefits of the change (in terms of increased revenue and reduced operational or overhead costs).

Maximize the Team's Ideas

HIGH IMPACT	NEGATIVE IMPACT
• Expressing appreciation of people's contributions to a suggestion box	• Giving the impression that no matter what ideas are offered they will not be implemented
• Making appropriate organizational changes based on a firm business case	• Implementing inappropriate ideas that have no sound business basis
• Allocating resources to the implementation of ideas	• Promising an implementation budget but failing to deliver

Case study: Avoiding Unnecessary Change

When Sanjeev was first promoted to the position of Sales and Marketing Director of his engineering firm, he was eager to make an impression by making some dramatic changes. He worked out a planning schedule and informed his manager, Serena, of his intentions. Serena asked him to come to see her and asked him two questions:

"Which is the most profitable organization in our sector?"

"Who is viewed as the market leader by most customers?"

Sanjeev knew that the answer to both questions was "We are," so he modified his plans.

• *Because Serena encouraged Sanjeev to think about how he was trying to create an impression by making changes for their own sake, she made sure that a successful operation did not falter under the burden of unnecessary change.*

• *By reviewing his plan, Sanjeev was able to look for the areas of the business where limited change would help to improve overall performance, leaving the main processes, products, and markets unchanged.*

Check the Appropriateness of Change

Good proactive team leaders have an appetite for change. They look for projects that they can put in place that have to do not with operational performance, but with improving the environment within which their team operates. Issuing laptops to the team, and encouraging them to work one or two days a week from home is a current trend. Do it only if you can see the return on the investment in computer hardware, for example, where improved job satisfaction reduces the rate of staff loss. In such a situation it is easy to underestimate the value of the staff interaction that occurs naturally when people are working in the same facility. Do not introduce change in areas that will have little impact on performance. Critically review the key drivers of team performance and identify room for improvement in those areas.

> **Change is inevitable in a progressive country.**
> **Change is constant.**
>
> Benjamin Disraeli

Avoid Half Measures

If your team has a significant problem, recognize that it will take a significant amount of effort to correct it and this may require a significant investment of resources. If, for example, a process such as the billing system is causing major problems, you may need to think about changing it entirely. Find the root cause of the problem, and determine to fix that rather than the symptoms. Do not forget that if you decide to make such a big change you will need money that doesn't come from your operational budget. If you instigate a series of change activities without getting the extra budget required you risk overloading people as they try to fit in the change activities around their normal operational responsibilities.

Will it Work? Ensure that any change in working practices will benefit the organization. Many people are well motivated and less distracted working from home; others need the interaction of an office environment to work well.

Summarize the Analysis

Your strategic plan will be based on your analysis of your current situation. Use a simple technique, SWOT analysis, to summarize your current position and turn the data you have gathered into information.

Use a SWOT Sheet

Bring the wealth of information you have gathered into a manageable summary using a SWOT (Strengths, Weaknesses, Opportunities, and Threats) sheet. You have already listed external trends, studied your customers and competitors, and reviewed your internal capabilities. The SWOT summary is a structured exercise that helps to clarify the team's views, acts as a powerful driver of the strategy, and provides a way of measuring progress as the team takes action to remove weaknesses and exploit opportunities. By listing your weaknesses you will identify key areas where you could improve performance and service. List as threats those external trends that, if

Understand your Team's SWOT

Write a series of simple statements as a summary of your current position, using sentences rather than bullet points to avoid misunderstandings. The statements should provide answers to the following questions:

→ **Strengths**—What is the team competent at doing? What activities is it really good at?

→ **Weaknesses**—Where is the team short of resources or capabilities? Where does it have competitive disadvantages?

→ **Opportunities**—How could the team boost its sales and improve its service? Where are there new markets to supply?

→ **Threats**—How might our products and services be overtaken? Which markets are deteriorating?

ignored, will damage your ability to succeed. In subsequent reviews of the SWOT analysis you will

Exploit Your Strengths A team that has a good awareness of its strengths and weaknesses will know how best to take advantage of its opportunities.

check that capabilities are listed correctly. A capability is either a strength or a weakness, depending on whether it contributes to the future strategy of the organization.

Share the Summary

Before you use the summary as a basis for your strategy, show it to your stakeholders so that they can point out any areas of misunderstanding or issues that are already being addressed by someone else in the organization. It may also be useful to share some of your summary with key customers. Look for ways in which you can use your strengths to remove your weaknesses, exploit your opportunities, and avoid or overcome threats. Having analyzed what is important to your customers, and having checked that they agree with your analysis, you can be confident that your final plan will be customer driven.

TIP **Assure the team members that they are an important part of future strategy and will produce a better plan if they are frank about their weaknesses.**

Summary: Staying Ahead

Look at the economic environment, analyze what your customers and other stakeholders need and want, check what your competition is doing, and establish what you and your team are capable of doing. Work out what you will have to change if you are to achieve success in the implementation of your strategic plan.

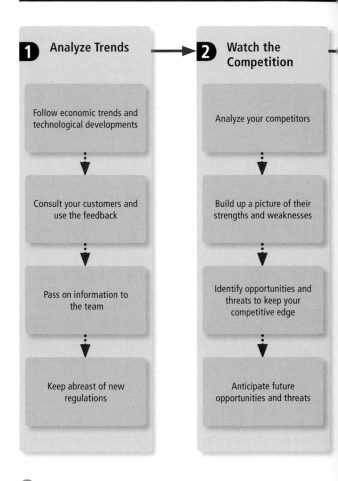

Looking at the Current Situation

1 Analyze Trends

Follow economic trends and technological developments

Consult your customers and use the feedback

Pass on information to the team

Keep abreast of new regulations

2 Watch the Competition

Analyze your competitors

Build up a picture of their strengths and weaknesses

Identify opportunities and threats to keep your competitive edge

Anticipate future opportunities and threats

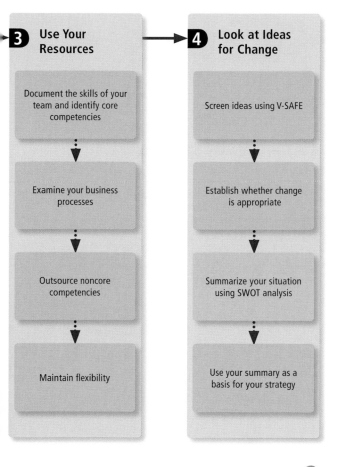

3 **Use Your Resources**

Document the skills of your team and identify core competencies

↓

Examine your business processes

↓

Outsource noncore competencies

↓

Maintain flexibility

4 **Look at Ideas for Change**

Screen ideas using V-SAFE

↓

Establish whether change is appropriate

↓

Summarize your situation using SWOT analysis

↓

Use your summary as a basis for your strategy

Create a
Strategic
Plan

3

Successful strategic thinkers use a logical process to define their strategy, moving from an overall statement of purpose to a clear statement of where they will focus their time and energies. This chapter shows you how to:

- Understand the unique contribution your team can make to your customers
- Set the boundaries of your operation—where the team will and will not work
- Choose strategic emphasis on products and markets and plan changes in focus
- Integrate your strategy with the rest of the organization and communicate it to everyone who needs to know about it

Stage the Process

Formulate your strategy in stages, involving the team and other stakeholders when appropriate. The decisions you make at each stage will give your strategy direction and a framework for future activities.

Remain Flexible

A strategic plan provides the environment in which the team will work. It is the key to a difficult dilemma in running a team or an organization—how can we be sure that the activities we engage in when pursuing a particular objective remain valid when things change? Suppose, for example, that you are the internal finance team of the distribution arm of a software organization, and that the divisional strategy is to market only its own products. If someone comes to you with a business case for becoming a channel for a competitive product, you could reference the strategy and decline the business case. If, however, sales of your organization's products are declining, you may want to reopen that part of the strategy for discussion and possible change. You give the strategy the chance to succeed but remain flexible about a dramatic change in circumstances.

Be Open To Change
As soon as the need for a change in the plan arises, discuss this with the team.

Check the Strategy

As part of the strategic planning process you will identify criteria that will be used to screen new products, services, or market areas. Together these form a template that can be used to provide a formal business case. This is used to test both current activities and future ideas to ascertain whether or not they will fit with your strategy. If, for example, a criterion is to keep service staff to a minimum, an idea for a new, high-maintenance product would not fit. You could either discard the idea or make it fit the template by altering the product or service, or by putting more resources into that market.

Agree on the Process

The first stage in a strategy is to define your goals. Once you understand what your purpose is you will be able to determine where

The Stages of Strategic Planning

Define Purpose
Create a definitive statement of future goals that all stakeholders agree to

Determine Advantage
Identify why customers will use your services rather than anyone else's

Set Boundaries
List all the products and markets you will deal in, and those in which you definitely will not

Choose Areas of Emphasis
Identify the focus of your resources by product and market

Integrate Stategy
Negotiate agreement on how to implement the plan and create process maps

your competitive edge lies, or what it is you have that is unique and that customers want. You will then need to set boundaries and choose areas on which you wish to focus, decide which stakeholders you wish to consult as you go through the process, and work out a time scale.

Define Your Purpose

Every part of an organization must have a purpose. Ask yourself why you exist, both in your own organization and in the outside world. Define your goals and agree on a statement of purpose to help you to focus.

Create a Statement of Purpose

When you begin to create a strategic plan, define your goals by discussing them with others, particularly your customers. Think about the wording of your statement of purpose, since this is the first boundary for the strategic plan and should help all stakeholders to understand where the strategy will lead. Ask your team for a succinct and clear statement of what it is going to deliver, to whom it will deliver, and how it will go about delivering it. Do not be tempted to write a "mission statement," because these tend to be long and somewhat vague and will not help in the creation of a strategic plan. Instead, make sure that the team creates a statement based on the research it has conducted with customers and competitors.

think SMART

When you agree on your statement of purpose, ask the team what they believe should be their reputation within the organization. This will help with the focus of the rest of the planning process.

For example, an IT department might add to its statement of purpose a branding statement: "We will be known throughout the organization as a department that concentrates on understanding our customers' business, rather than one that tries to explain its business to its customers." The addition of such a specific declaration to the statement of purpose is often referred to as "branding the team," and helps contribute to the team's sense of identity within the organization.

Improve Your Statement of Purpose

When you have written your first draft test it for its strengths. A strong statement of purpose leaves no room for doubt about what you and your team are going to do. Establish whether your statement does this by imagining the questions that the current statement could give rise to:

→ **Weak first draft:** "We will concentrate on exploiting our considerable experience in food products."
→ **Leaves open the question:** "Will you only be selling products and where do you intend to send them?"
→ **Stronger statement of purpose:** "We will supply food products and services to North American markets, mainly Canada, in the first two years of our overseas operation."

Communicate your Statement of Purpose

Your team, like all the others in the organization, needs good links with other teams to operate effectively. Make sure that your team is absolutely clear about what its purpose is, as defined in the statement of purpose. It is important that no one is planning to operate outside it. Ensure that the team understands how its purpose fits in with the other teams within the organization and that it appreciates the goals of the cross-functional teams with which it has dealings. Some organizations have formal structures in place for the communication of strategic goals to staff, but if one does not exist it will be up to you to ensure that your team's goals are made widely known. Use this sharing of goals as an opportunity to foster good relations with other teams working within the organization.

The statement of purpose needs the support of the whole team

Determine Advantage

Whatever your team does that sets it apart will be a principal driver of your strategy. Review your analysis and create a statement that clearly sums up what your competitive advantage is.

Agree on what Your Customers Want from You

All organizations and teams have unique capabilities and resources; however, these do not always translate into providing an advantage to your customers. Ask yourself three key questions to identify the unique contribution that your team brings to the organization and your customers:

- Do your customers and markets actually want the products and services you are providing in the way that you are providing them?
- Do you know what your customers' needs and wants are?
- Are there some products and services that you should drop?
- Are there any gaps that you could fill?

Use "So What" to Find the Benefits

Competitive advantage feature—customers can enter their own orders online.

SO WHAT?

As soon as customers realize that they are running short of stock they can place an order.

SO WHAT?

This reduces the threat of being out of stock.

SO WHAT?

Customer benefit—without this feature the customer will lose sales.

Predict the Future

Looking at historic trends can help to confirm whether you will still thrive in the future, but it won't anticipate changes that come from unexpected sources. Consider whether

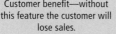

what helps you to thrive in business today will allow you to survive tomorrow. Ask whether customers will still want your products and services tomorrow, and whether you will still be performing more effectively and efficiently than your competitors or alternatives sources of supply in the future. If the answer is "no," you need to change. Many organizations and teams disappear within the first 12 months of starting up their operation because they stopped anticipating the changes in their environment. Check that any advantage will survive into at least year two of your strategy. If you believe, for example, that people are your main source of competitive advantage, ask yourself how you will protect that advantage.

Keep Ahead Having identified what it is that gives you your competitive advantage, work out whether you will need to make any changes in order to retain that advantage and succeed in your strategy.

What Gives You a Competitive Advantage?

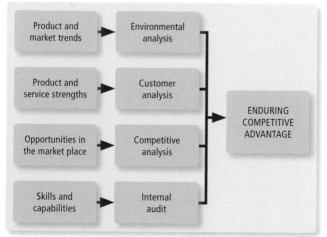

Product and market trends	→	Environmental analysis
Product and service strengths	→	Customer analysis
Opportunities in the market place	→	Competitive analysis
Skills and capabilities	→	Internal audit

ENDURING COMPETITIVE ADVANTAGE

Set Boundaries

As you implement your strategy you will come under pressure to meet new demands. Define parameters so that the team is clear about what it will focus on and ensure that everyone has agreed to your boundaries.

Maintain Focus

Setting clear boundries prevents people from wasting time and energy responding to demands that fall outside the remit of the strategic plan. It is impossible to predict and plan for every eventuality from the outset, and many of the choices that occur later in the planning process are likely to offer genuine and worthwhile opportunities. Attempting to do too much, however, will spread resources too thinly and dilute the focus and effectiveness of your strategy. By setting the boundries for future action at the outset of the strategic planning process, you can ensure that everyone concentrates on the key points of the strategy and you avoid any sort of "mission creep."

Case study: Saving Resources

Gianni, an account manager for an IT outsourcing company, was under pressure from Catherine, one of his customers, who wanted Gianni's company to support a website that she was using for a business process template. Gianni's boss, Damian, pointed out to him that the boundaries set at the beginning of the planning process specifically did not allow supporting websites on out-of-house servers. Damian suggested that they go to Catherine and explain their strategy. Catherine accepted the logic. She was interested not only in the boundaries, but also in the planning process itself, and Gianni agreed to supply her with a document to show how to develop a strategic plan.

• *By remaining within their boundaries, Damian and Gianni avoided the considerable expense and risk of using an out-of-house server.*
• *By being open about their planning process they had strengthened their relationship with Catherine.*

Set Down Boundaries Clearly
Make sure the parameters are set and discussed during a team meeting so that everyone is in agreement.

If any team members have a pet project for a new ideas that they believe will benefit the customer, they must try to sell the idea to the team. If the team views this idea as irrelevent and rejects it, the team members must be prepared to accept that boundary—which is why it is vital to gain consensus on boundaries at an early stage.

Target the Right Set of Customers

It is very natural for team members to want to react to new customers and promise them service. Understanding where the boundaries are is vital in this area as well. Draw up a list of the markets you will sell to and the markets that you will not address without a change in the situation and in your strategy. Make it clear that exceptions to the boundaries will not be allowed without justification.

TIP **Choosing customers who will be there for the long term may cost money in the short term, but it will ensure the long-term viability of the team.**

Choose Areas of Emphasis

Your choice of strategic emphasis will tell you where to put your resources and where your people should spend their time. To get these priorities right, look at your products, services, and markets in appropriate groups.

Segment Markets and Customers

Group your markets and customers to make the list more manageable. This is an opportunity for the team to be creative and possibly come up with new insights for new markets. Think of the first bank to realize that there was a huge group of customers who wanted to do their banking online, or the first airline that anticipated the massive growth in customers who would prefer a cheaper ticket price to any form of luxury during the trip.

5 minute FIX

If the team is spending too much time debating into which groups they should put products:

- Put an important product into the first group, then add products that the team feels should be in the same group

- Add a new group if a product doesn't fit into any of the existing groups

- Identify the common theme for each group.

Group Products and Services

Exploring creative options for groups can often spark off new ideas in a planning session. If you have many products and services you will find them easier to manage if you consider them in groups when deciding which are the most important. Group by:

- **Complexity**—A simple group might need little after-sales support while a complex one may require a lot of support

- **Value**—You may want to consider focusing on high value/low volume products

- **Maturity**—You may wish to place products that you have been selling for a while in one group and put new products in another.

Establish Priorities

In order to identify which groups of products and services are important for today's revenues, and which are going to be important in the long term, examine potential sales volumes and values over the next two to three years.

Do the same thing in terms of markets and estimate the current and future sales revenues and/or profits of each of these groupings. Think about how you can be successful with each group of markets by recognizing what the market is looking for. Imagine, for example, that you're a food distribution company:

→ What services will your customers need in the long term? Their main emphasis may be on price, so you might have to think of ways to keep the production costs down.

→ What else might change? Customers may decide to introduce a policy of using local suppliers, reducing the "air miles" of the food products they sell.

→ What demands will new products make on your investment resources? You may have to think about changing to an automatic packing system.

→ In what way will you have to improve your service with these products? Faster distribution will make sure that you maintain your sales of this group.

The information you obtain during this process will help you to establish priorities. It will also help you to recognize gaps in your capabilities for achieving the strategy. Exploring creative options in groups will often spark off new ideas in a planning session.

Remember that nothing ever stays the same, so it is important to review your reviewing process frequently. A reviewing process that has worked for some time may not suit changed circumstances.

TIP **Always document your planning discussions comprehensively; you may find that you need to refer to the detail of earlier debates later on.**

Agree on What the Emphasis Should Be

Each member of the team must agree on where the strategic emphasis should be. A split in focus can cause conflict and adversely affect performance. This is particularly true when members of the team come from different parts of the organization. People who deal directly with customers may believe that the focus should be on products that are easy to sell, while those working to produce a more complex range of products may insist that the concentration should be on those products because they are more profitable. Check that your manager and other stakeholders support your strategic emphasis. This will help you to secure their agreement on the resources that you will need to have in place if your plan is to be successfully implemented.

Resolve Anomalies

As circumstances change and you review your emphasis, you may notice anomalies and discover areas that no longer deserve so many resources for a decreasing return. And, of course, new opportunities will occur. Resolve these anomalies by:

→ Planning to reduce the amount of effort in declining areas and taking resources away from them before the sales value becomes insufficient to pay for the people who are working on that product/market.
→ Striking while the iron is hot if you see an area of good potential, and putting in more resources to create the necessary competitive advantage.

Timing and communication are key when you are dealing with changed circumstances. Plan ahead and reallocate resources at the best possible time. Communicating the product/market matrix throughout the organization or department contributes toward a cross-functional, "we are all one team" view.

Document Your Product/Market Emphasis

Devise a product/market matrix showing where you plan to upgrade and reduce emphasis on a product/market. This matrix will enable everyone to understand the team's intentions.

	Market A	Market B	Market C
Product 1	Now: High level of activity Goal: Low level of activity	Now: Medium level of activity Goal: Low level of activity	Now: Low level of activity Goal: High level of activity
Product 2	Now: Medium level of activity Goal: High level of activity	Now: No activity at all Goal: Medium level of activity	Now: No activity at all Goal: Medium level of activity

Change Emphasis When Necessary

You cannot sell a product unless you have a market to sell it into; similarly, you have no interest in a market for which you have no appropriate product. Think in terms of product/markets—segments of the market that your products are suited to. As products change or markets begin to take on new characteristics, you may have to change emphasis in each product/market segment. How often you have to do this depends on the volatility of your product/markets.

- If a customer group is putting weight on low prices, you may choose to downgrade the resources and effort you are putting into that product/market, and withdraw from that segment over time.
- Change is very rapid in some sectors—organizations that supply software, for example, may find that they have to review their strategic emphasis twice a year. In contrast, in the steel industry, emphasis would need to be reviewed only occasionally.

Integrate Strategy

You set out on the planning process with a clear understanding of your organization's strategy. Check that in choosing, for example, product/market emphasis, your strategy still fits into the organization as a whole.

Identify Conflict

If strategic thinking is not common practice throughout your organization, you may unintentionally reveal outmoded and ineffective methods in the operations of some other teams. Act sensitively. Consider whether other teams in the organization will understand what you are trying to do and the changes you are trying to make. Be sure you can argue for these changes strongly before you discuss them with other team leaders. Work out a mutually acceptable way ahead and always be prepared to compromise as you move along. If you cannot initiate a new process while an old one remains in place for other teams, work out how to rectify the situation.

- Open negotiations with other teams and stimulate thoughts of change and improvement.
- Discuss matters with your peers and put forward the idea of a planning cycle, where each team reviews each other's plans at different stages.

Negotiate Agreement
If you need to make some controversial changes to working practices, work these out with the people involved.

Align Strategies

If your organization does not currently standardize the formulation of strategic plans, you could always suggest a simple step-by-step approach. Computer systems, for example, have a vital role to play in standardization. They allow organizations to communicate and update their plans online. The most successful organizations do not have impenetrable walls between departments. They document their processes, noting where and when the different teams are required to get involved and helping these teams to follow an agreed upon strategy.

Prepare Process Maps

When projects or operational systems involve different teams, use a process map to identify where each stage of a process moves from one team to another. The danger points to projects or systems lie at the different handover stages, where delays and misunderstandings may occur. To avoid problems, make sure that each team sees its own part in the process in the context of everyone else's. Teams working independently, without any reference to what other teams are doing, will endanger the long-term success of the strategy and the achievement of the goals of the organization.

Map Business Processes

Use a diagram to map how a process moves between departments.

Handover to the Sales Team, which considers where and how much it could sell, and the price

Handover to Production, which assesses viability and price and produces a report

Handover to Product Development, which produces a project plan

Handover to Sales Team, which gets feedback from customers and focus groups

Summary: Getting it Right

The key to creating the right strategic plan is to take your team with you. Go through a formal process to establish what the unique qualities of your team are. Decide what the parameters of the strategy are and narrow your target down to the best possible plan for achieving your purpose. Put in place a process for implementing the plan.

Finding a Balance

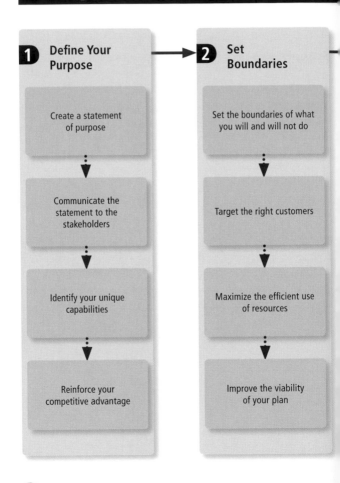

1 Define Your Purpose

Create a statement of purpose

⬇

Communicate the statement to the stakeholders

⬇

Identify your unique capabilities

⬇

Reinforce your competitive advantage

2 Set Boundaries

Set the boundaries of what you will and will not do

⬇

Target the right customers

⬇

Maximize the efficient use of resources

⬇

Improve the viability of your plan

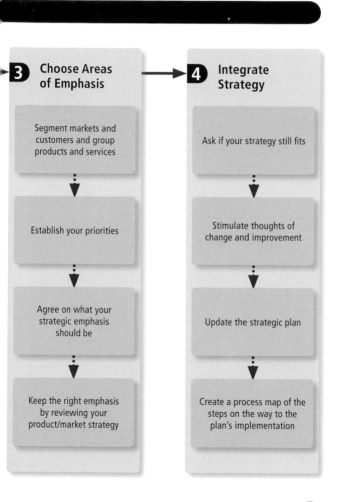

3 Choose Areas of Emphasis → **4** Integrate Strategy

Choose Areas of Emphasis

Segment markets and customers and group products and services

↓

Establish your priorities

↓

Agree on what your strategic emphasis should be

↓

Keep the right emphasis by reviewing your product/market strategy

Integrate Strategy

Ask if your strategy still fits

↓

Stimulate thoughts of change and improvement

↓

Update the strategic plan

↓

Create a process map of the steps on the way to the plan's implementation

Estimate a Budget

A key measure of the success of a strategy is the achievement of its financial goals. Look at potential sources of income and revenues and estimate future costs to arrive at an overall budget.

Forecast Income

Forecast income in detail for the first year and in outline for the next two years. Even if there is a lot of uncertainty in your forecast, write it down and then revise it frequently as real figures become available. Think it through, because not doing so puts you at risk of producing an unrealistic plan. If you underestimate demand for your services you will not be able to supply it; if you overestimate demand you will not meet the profit target you set yourself in the budget. Look at the forecast in terms of optimistic, most likely, and pessimistic outcomes for each product/market. In the end, the forecast of what you commit yourself to sell or supply drives all the other internal budgets.

Set Out a Budget

Expenditure	Year 1	Year 2	Year 3
People	33,500	36,850	40,535
Supplies	22,000	24,200	26,620
Facilities	12,000	13,200	14,520
Equipment	6,500	7,150	7,865
Information	2,500	2,750	3,025
Total expenditure	76,500	84,150	92,565
Total income	102,000	121,000	139,000
Forecast profit	**25,500**	**36,850**	**46,435**

TIP When you have made your budget, reduce income or sales revenue by half and work out what you would do if that were to be the case in reality.

Become Numerate

Accounting is not a natural talent for everyone, but in order to plan and follow through a strategy successfully, it is vital to have a good understanding of the basics of budgeting and forecasting. If you are weak in this area take steps to fill the knowledge gap, by taking a course or reading the financial pages of newspapers. Once you understand the principles of accounting budgeting will become easier with practice.

A realistic estimate will produce a realistic budget

Estimate Costs

From your forecast and your knowledge of your customers you can make a fairly accurate estimate of the costs involved in implementing your strategy. Generally, it is useful to break down costs into five categories:

→ **People**—The total cost of the staff that will be involved in implementing the strategy.

→ **Supplies**—The cost of all the materials, products, and other items you will have to buy in to service your customers.

→ **Facilities**—The internal or external charges that you will pay for space and other facilities.

→ **Equipment**—A summary of the charges for all the equipment and technology you will rent or buy.

→ **Information**—The cost of administration and research.

You may need the help of other stakeholders in making this estimate. For example, you may need to know what you will be charged by the IT department for information services over the next three years. Concentrate on getting numbers that are realistic. Do not be too concerned about very detailed accuracy. It is an estimate and will need to be reviewed.

Test the Strategy

Once you have devised your strategic plan, it will generally stand until actual events require you to revise it or make modifications. Testing helps you identify at an earlier stage whether modifications will be required.

Build a Business Case Template

A business case template allows you to test whether a new product, service, or market idea will fit into the overall strategy. To create the template, list the most important criteria of your strategy. One criterion, for example, might be to maximize short-term sales, another to operate within the existing team's resources. Give each criterion a rating out of 10 that reflects its importance, with 10 being the highest priority. That gives the weighting you will attach to that criterion when you measure new ideas against it. For each criterion define the "ideal" case. In the sales case, you may ideally want any new idea to add 20 percent

Assess Importance Establish the importance of each criterion to the strategic plan and rank it accordingly in your business case template.

What is Most Important?

CRITERION	List the main criteria of your strategy
RATING	Rate the relative importance of each criterion on a scale of 1–10
IDEAL CASE	Measure the rating against the ideal scenario rating
STRATEGIC FIT	Multiply the weighting by the score to test the strategic fit

Test a New Idea

To find out how close a new idea is to your strategy you need a measure of "strategic fit." Convert the score achieved by the idea to a percentage and compare that with your ideal.

→ Multiply the priority rating of each criterion by your new idea rating. Add the weighted scores to give the ideal weighting.

→ Calculate the ideal weighting. The ideal rating is 10, so multiply each priority rating by 10 and calculate the total.

→ Calculate the strategic fit by working out what percentage of the total scores is the weighted score, in this example 61%.

→ This percentage tells you that the idea is a reasonable but not perfect strategic fit, and also gives you a single number to compare it against other ideas.

Calculate the Strategic Fit of a New Idea

Main strategy criteria	Priority rating (1–10)	New idea rating (0-10)	Weighted score	Ideal weighting (Priority x 10)
Increase short-term sales	7	7	49	70
Protect long-term sales	5	2	10	50
Keep staff to a minimum	7	8	56	70
Total scores			**115**	**190**
% of ideal				61%

to short-term sales. If the forecast is that short-term sales will increase by 10 percent then you could mark it five out of 10 against the ideal. Multiply this score by the priority of the criterion and you get the weighted score. This allows you, in a single percentage figure, to compare and prioritize a new product, service, or market idea, as well as ensuring a good strategic fit. You can use the business case template to test change project activities.

Manage Your Brand

It is your reputation as a team while you implement your strategy that locks in your customers and attracts new ones. Agree on your team values and manage people's perception of you as though it were your brand.

Set Your Values

Ask yourself, "What do I want people to think and feel when they hear my team's name or see its logo? What image am I trying to promote?" Talk to your team about this and agree on a set of values that describes the way you will go about providing your products and services: supportive, knowledgeable, innovative, hard-working. These words are the indicators of your brand. Remember, while a strong brand image is not a substitute for quality, it is certainly an enhancement of it.

Case study: Changing Your Image

Caroline, the director of HR in a technology company, found that team leaders had always called Mei Lee, the recruitment adviser, to a recruiting situation too late, making their own decisions on job descriptions and the type of person they were looking for. This meant that Mei Lee could not add her expertise and often found herself working with an unsuitable specification. Caroline did some research and found that managers in the field saw HR as an unnecessary nuisance that did not really contribute to the bottom line. Caroline and her team redefined their values, and persuaded their customers to see them as "enablers"—people who could help them to succeed with any project that required hiring new staff.

• *By researching their current image, the HR department had discovered why functional managers were using HR expertise in a way that did not maximize their contribution to overall performance.*
• *By getting the team to agree on their values and image, Caroline had shown what would make the department successful.*

Manage Perceptions

Create your brand by acting according to your values and giving your customers the experience you want them to have. Once you have agreed what you want the brand to stand for, work out how you are currently viewed by doing some research with customers and suppliers. Set your "visual image." If your visual image does not reflect branding, think about restyling it. Choose a logo that echoes the values of the brand. Think about how your people dress and make sure their whole behavior pushes forward the image you have decided upon. Remind the team that brands are a mixture of reality, good and bad performance, and perceptions. A good performance shouldn't be negated by poor perceptions.

5 minute FIX

If you take over a team with a poor reputation, you need to show customers that things are really going to change.

- Talk to three key customers and ask them what have been their main concerns over the last year.
- Decide how you can introduce change in the problem area that will demonstrate your commitment to improving your service in the future.

Promote a Good Image

HIGH IMPACT

- Having a logo that conveys your values and tells people something about what you do
- Checking product names with customers everywhere to make sure that they convey the right image where they are sold
- Communicating your brand by giving guidelines to anyone who is connected with the brand

NEGATIVE IMPACT

- Having an abstract logo that is not obviously connected with your operation
- Having a product name that has negative connotations in some parts of the country or world
- Allowing some parts of your operation to promote a different image from the one that has been centrally agreed upon

Communicate Clearly

If your strategy is to succeed, everyone who needs to understand it must be informed. Communicate your plan to every stakeholder so that they understand what the strategy does for them, and gain their commitment to it.

Use Appropriate Language

Keep the language you use simple and concise and define all the important words. Do not forget that simple words, such as "sales," can have different meanings in different contexts, so make sure that everyone understands the definition that your strategy uses.

Get Feedback

However you choose to communicate with stakeholders make sure that there is a mechanism for receiving feedback. This feedback will give you invaluable information on how the strategy impacts on stakeholders. The salespeople will be able to let you know how they think customers will react to your strategy and then tell you their actual experience as they meet directly with them. Site engineers can give you an insider's view of progress. Do not react defensively to feedback.

think
SMART

Remember that many people do not read an entire written communication thoroughly. Make sure that if they read only the first couple of paragraphs of a document they will still get the point.

List any actions that they are required to do in the first paragraph, and describe the main benefit to them in the second paragraph. Then, even if someone fails to read the entire document, you will still achieve your objective because you have included the main points at the beginning.

Communicate the Strategy

It is important to brief stakeholders succinctly and appropriately. You should choose the correct medium of communication and tell the right things to the right people:

→ **Superiors and team members**—These are the only people to whom you should send the detailed plan in full. Include the analysis information to back up the decisions you have made.

→ **Other stakeholders**—Produce a personalized extract from the detailed report to meet their needs.

→ **Team members, internal stakeholders, and your manager's peer group**—These groups will probably benefit from a presentation of the strategy. The presentation should motivate the audience to give feedback then and there and to read the detailed or outline report after the meeting.

Properly targeted information will hit the mark

→ **Stakeholders in the long term**— A newsletter that records your progress against the plan will keep them up to date. Keep the newsletters brief and send them out to people only when you have something new to say.

→ **Large numbers of stakeholders with a limited interest in the strategy**—This group may only need an email or a letter from time to time to keep it up to date.

As with all communications, check regularly that people have understood. Ask what action they will take as a result of the change in strategy—this will not only initiate the necessary changes but also test for understanding and commitment.

TIP Never hold back from communicating your plans to stakeholders because you are concerned that they will not like all or part of the strategy.

Implement 4
the Strategic
Plan

Creating the strategic plan is an exciting
part of the strategic thinking process, but
the benefits of the plan will be realized only
through a well-disciplined and methodical
implementation. This chapter will help you to:

- Set priorities to make the best use of
  the team's time
- Plan the activities necessary to change
  how you operate
- Form appropriate strategic partnerships
- Lead your team effectively by motivating
  it to drive the plan to completion
- Monitor and review your success to date,
  and maintain the relevance and dynamism
  of the strategy

Prioritize Change

In addition to achieving the short-term operational goals defined in your plan, you and your team must decide which changes to current methods of work must be put in place to ensure you achieve the long-term strategy.

Make a List of Possible Improvements

Draw up a comprehensive list of possibilities for changing how you operate, grouping them into separate areas for improvement. Changes in the strategy with regard to products and markets will drive this list, as well as changes in the way you are going to operate to achieve improvements in effectiveness. This list becomes the starting point for your decisions on change projects. Use your team to make sure the list is comprehensive. Remember that at this time you are not making decisions on change projects but figuring out what needs to be done and what the priorities are.

Case study: Identifying the Problem

During the prioritization stage of the strategic plan, Bill's team put a very high urgency on changing their mailing lists from residential prospects to corporations. Only Freddie stood out against what seemed to be a necessary change. During a break Bill took Freddie aside and asked him what was troubling him about making the switch. It became clear that Freddie, whose job it was to write the direct mail leaflets, was not at all confident that he knew how to write to companies rather than individuals. Bill told Freddie that he would arrange for him to attend an internal training course to bring his skills up to speed.

• By detecting that something was holding Freddie back from agreeing with the team on the necessary change, Bill had identified the problem and was able to address it.
• By talking to Freddie outside the full team session and suggesting a way forward, Bill was able to persuade Freddie to agree to the change and the team was able to move ahead with its plan.

Make the Right Changes

HIGH IMPACT

- Putting emphasis where it is needed even if it will prove difficult to make the changes
- Handling high impact areas early
- Taking external influences into account but resolving to make the necessary changes
- Taking considered risks

NEGATIVE IMPACT

- Resolving to introduce improvements only in areas that are easy to change rather than those that have a serious impact
- Waiting to respond to a crisis
- Making external influences the major driver of the plan
- Choosing the safest option

Set Priorities

In order to reach a decision about how to prioritize the change projects, list each area for improvement and label it high, medium, or low in terms of impact and urgency. You will have no option but to deal with the issues that have high impact and high urgency first. Use the measure to prioritize the changes, and then group them so that you arrive at between eight and ten areas for change. These groupings will be the basis of the change projects. As you implement your strategy, the team members will gradually become more proactive and find that they are working on high impact changes before they become high urgency. Changes that offer a quick, tangible result make people realize that change is actually happening. However, you should resist the temptation to label everything as high priority. Drop some nonessential activities by making hard but realistic decisions. Your resources are

Aim for the ideal but be prepared to settle for less

finite, and these change projects often have to be performed by the members of the team in addition to their normal operational tasks. It's important not to compromise the objectives of the organization.

Form Strategic Partnerships

A major change in how organizational strategies are created has been the dramatic growth in outsourcing and forming other types of strategic partnership in order to streamline operations.

Outsource Processes

It is possible to describe any organization as a series of strategic partnerships between the different functions that provide services to each other. For example, the planning teams might have realized that there were two good reasons for making other departments compete with outside contractors to provide the same service.

- By moving some of the less strategic activities out of the organization they were able to concentrate their attention on the core business and make better use of the available resources.
- By outsourcing some activities they were able to get a better performance from the new supplier since the contracts and agreements were better defined and roles and responsibilities were more finely understood.

Take this growth of outsourcing seriously when developing your strategy. Look creatively for those parts of your

think
SMART

Never simply accept that an internal department that supplies you with a service has to continue to do this if you could get a better or cheaper service externally.

Challenge your internal suppliers—if you find a more cost-effective alternative to one of your suppliers you are not only improving your performance, but also the performance of the whole organization. This is true whether you go outside for the service, or if, as a direct result of your challenge, your internal supplier improves its cost-effectiveness.

operation that would be better served from outside the organization. Understand what makes you special and concentrate on that. Consider how your internal customers are measuring your performance to make sure that you are part of their own long-term strategy.

Consider OEM Product

Globalization has had an enormous impact on OEM (original equipment manufacturer) product strategies. Organizations asked themselves why it was necessary to manufacture their products in their own production facilities. If there is a cheaper source, albeit on the other side of the world, does it not make sense to take advantage of that? Ask yourself broad questions about your operation and where some of it could be outsourced and rebranded under your logo. However, steer clear of outsourcing to achieve a cost saving to the detriment of customer service. Outsourcing a call center facility may be a financially beneficial strategy; but if the operatives are talking to your customers in a language that is not their first language, or that is spoken with a dialect or accent that makes it difficult for your customers to understand, there could be a backlash of customer dissatisfaction.

Types of Supplier Partnerships

Strategic Suppliers
who are involved in
our strategic plan

**Preferred
Suppliers**
with whom all teams
should work

Commodity Suppliers
who are chosen by price
and availability

Which Group? Their position on the pyramid indicates the relative size of each group of suppliers. Here, the smallest group, the strategic suppliers, is at the top of the pyramid. The largest group is that formed by the commodity suppliers.

Outsource Sales

Look Outside You may benefit from outsourcing activities for which you don't have the skills base.

The principle of partnering and outsourcing can also apply to sales and marketing activities. It is the skill of a salesperson that ensures that current and prospective customers understand and accept your proposal. Some teams and even some businesses do not have that key skill available to them. Consider using specialized organizations to manage key aspects of the selling process. You could use them to do market research, or to define your solution to a customer's problem.

TECHNIQUES *to* practice

A very useful skill to develop is the ability to identify quickly the culture of an organization.
Look at your own organization and at any other organization with which you come into contact. Get into the habit of asking people about the culture in their organization:

- What balance do you have between quality and cost?
- Are people free to operate in their own way or do they have to work within strict processes and controls?
- Do teams work independently and without reference to each other or is there a tradition of sharing information?

Look for New Channels

It is likely that your strategy will include a move into a new market or new markets. In such cases there is a long learning curve while your team figures out how the people in the new market operate. A shortcut could be provided by another organization already selling into that market. They have had to learn how to address the market themselves, and you may be able to piggyback on their knowledge. Check if it makes sense to sell to new markets through these alternative channels. You may find that you will sell at lower margins but increase sales and profits.

Form Joint Marketing Initiatives

Look for organizations or teams where your products and services have a high synergy. Traditional partnerships, such as those between publishers and business schools are being joined by less obvious initiatives, for example, software, training, and consulting firms, combining to provide a total solution from one source. Be careful, though, to make sure that there is a good strategic fit between the organizations involved.

→ Are the two cultures aligned? There are many examples of businesses going through very difficult times when they merged or worked together because of a clash of cultures, with neither side understanding how the other side operated.

→ Are the skills and capabilities of each of the parties complementary? It is vital to be working jointly rather than competing with one another.

A well-thought-through joint initiative can pay huge dividends to the parties involved as they save costs, exploit each other's brand presence, and move more swiftly to good performance. It can work internally as well with, for example, the legal and commercial departments of an organization providing a combined service to its internal customers.

Plan Change Activities

People may resist changing the way they go about doing their work, and activities that promote change tend to be an addition to everyone's workload. Work out detailed action plans for all your change projects.

Define Objectives

Before deciding on an action plan, make sure that you have defined exactly what each change project is trying to achieve and by when. Make the objectives as tight and as specific as possible and ensure that they conform to SMART, a useful acronym that defines objectives as:

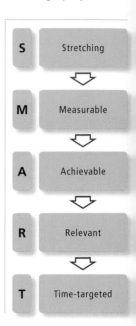

- **Stretching**—The objectives must be challenging, to make sure that the team operates at maximum efficiency.
- **Measurable**—The objectives must be quantifiable so that you can check if you have achieved them.
- **Achievable**—The objectives must be achievable.
- **Relevant**—The objectives should be relevant to your customers and improve your service to them.
- **Time-targeted**—The objectives must have an end date.

Set Milestones

Define a set of milestones—events or achievements that demonstrate that you are moving toward the objective—so that the team can check that the change project is on track. Ask yourself what steps are required to get to each milestone. A milestone might be an event, such as the production of a report, or an achievement, such as getting a commitment to the allocation of resources.

Change Project Action Plan

A clear statement of the overall project purpose	**Purpose** To implement a new order processing system within a budget of $50,000		
SMART objectives and clear measures of success	**Objectives and measures** • A reduction in our debt collection period from an average of 80 days to 50 days • A reduction in the number of customer inquiries from 100 per month to 20 per month		
	Major phases	**Timescales**	**Responsible**
A person is given responsibility for implementation and given a clear date to aim for	Pilot system in place in southern region	By end January next year	Area manager
	Full implementation	By September	Area manager
An event or achievement marking the progress made toward a change project objective	Milestones		
	Customer contact system agreed by at least two major customers	End of May	Sales manager
	Recommendation agreed by the board	June board meeting	Sales manager

TIP Ensure that your team takes its participation in change projects as seriously as it does its delivery of products to customers on time.

List Actions

Take each project milestone and break it down into a series of actions with estimated start and end dates. Make sure that the dates you decide on take into account your operational plans and short-term targets. However, as change projects improve the working environment, you may have to review some operating procedures to fit in with the new environment. Now list the projects along with their key timescale milestones and make sure that they fit together well. This list will change as the project proceeds, reflecting the progress you are making with your portfolio of change projects.

TIP People are most easily motivated by a direct instruction from their manager.

Case study: Allocating Responsibility

Alan, a senior team member in logistics, was having trouble implementing a new distribution system. The problems arose when he needed input from the sales force. He would send a note to all the salespeople, reminding them that they were due to comment on a proposal or provide input from customer research, but no one got back to him. He discussed the problem with Leah, the sales manager. When she looked at the project documentation she saw that Alan had allocated responsibility to the "sales team" and suggested that he put the names of individual salespeople beside each action.

As soon as Alan started doing this the members of the sales team started to respond to him.

• *By removing any ambiguity about who was responsible for each action Alan had ensured that the individuals took their actions more seriously and gave him the necessary information when he needed it.*
• *By getting the agreement of Leah to the list of responsible people Alan had put more pressure on the sales team to carry out their part of the change project.*

Perform Change Activities Effectively

Change projects can be tricky to implement because nobody really likes to do things differently and many people resist changing the way they operate.

Keep the Focus
When progress is difficult, people may revert to concentrating on operational tasks. Explain to them the importance of the change project to them and to the organization.

Give Responsibility
It is vital that someone takes responsibility for each milestone. This person will not necessarily be responsible for the actions needed to get to the milestone.

Allocate Actions
Allocate someone to perform each action that will take you to the milestone. This person will report to the individual who is ultimately responsible for the milestones.

Set Timescales

Achieving change takes time. However, if, for example, the change is urgent but the problem has little short-term

Motivate the Team It is not just mountaineers who must rely on teammates for success—make it clear that your team must work together in order to reach its target.

impact, there is a danger that members of the team will put a low priority on their part in the change project action list. By setting time targets and agreeing on them with the person responsible, you will ensure that she will not be sidetracked by everyday operational issues. Emphasize to the team that failure to change now will seriously hurt the performance of the team in the future. If people have agreed to achievable timescales they will be highly motivated.

Look for Shortcuts

Look at the list of actions for each project and ask yourself, "Is there any way we could achieve this objective more quickly?" For example:

- Perhaps you could get an external organization to implement the changes more quickly
- If another internal team is planning to make the same change, perhaps they could lead the way and save you some time and resources

Try to make use of people's knowledge and previous experience to help in current and future change projects.

A member of your team may have relevant experience from a previous organization, for example. Listen carefully and do not resist an approach that is different from the one you had in mind. Take steps to ensure that your team and any other teams that are facing a similar problem can learn from successes in the past.

- Identify other projects, both historic and current, that might have relevance to how you manage the new project.
- Update progress notes frequently, focusing on things that happened and why they happened.
- Make these notes available to the members of the team.
- Ask other teams to keep and share similar records.

- Check if anyone else in your organization, or in any other team that you are involved with, has made a similar change before. Borrow her project plan and notes and ask her to meet you or the whole team to discuss how she made the improvement
- Make sure that at least 20 percent of the people whose tasks will change are committed and motivated to assist in the achievement of the objectives. These agents of change will be very helpful in gaining the agreement of people who are less eager to welcome the challenge of the changes you want to make.

Some organizations develop a file of "insights," short statements of what they have learned in operational or change activities. Sorted into categories, such as finance or distribution, these can prove invaluable in facing future problems and opportunities.

Change for the sake of change should be avoided

The First 100 Days

Having set a strategy and identified change projects, real success follows when you implement it on time and within budget. However long a period the overall plan needs to cover, it is vital to get off to a flying start.

Make Sure the Strategy is Right

A good start gives your team, your managers, and other stakeholders confidence that you can make your strategy work. In the first 100 days concentrate on fine-tuning the plan into a robust tool that everyone understands and supports. You may need to meet once a week during this initial period to make sure that what seemed feasible at the time of planning remains feasible once people have started to perform the first parts of the action plan. Emphasize the removal of obstacles to implementation.

Discuss the Need for Change

Use the review meetings to listen to views and to communicate plans and progress. When all the team members have access to information they are in a better position to make decisions quickly. Explain what you have had to change and why you had to change it. Suppose, for example, that the plan envisioned reducing the emphasis on a particular product; you have decided to promote a new product instead. However, when you inform your customers of this change they threaten to reduce orders in the product area that you are trying to expand. You may have to revise the plan to keep your market share.

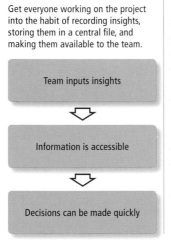

Share Insights

Get everyone working on the project into the habit of recording insights, storing them in a central file, and making them available to the team.

Team inputs insights

⬇

Information is accessible

⬇

Decisions can be made quickly

Record Progress

During review meetings look critically at places where you are off track. See what effect this will have on the plan, alter the plan accordingly, and make a good record of what has happened. Avoid, however, making review meetings a long list of bad news. Make a record of where you have had success as well: nothing breeds success better than success. Create a master file of all the action and resource plans. Include as an appendix the research that was conducted during the analysis stage. Keep the data practical. Refer back to the file frequently and encourage your team to do the same. The goal is to keep the document dynamic and up to date.

Keep Up to Date Make sure that your strategy is keeping up with changes in your customers' requirements—discuss this regularly with the team.

Assess Risks

Having tested the strategy for problems at the planning stage, look at the change project plans to establish what might prevent them from succeeding. List the risks and, if necessary, alter the plans to minimize them.

Predict Problems

Ask the team to brainstorm and come up with a list of potential threats and future problems. Look at each plan and ask, "What could prevent this from happening?" Encourage people to treat problems as just another challenge of implementing change. If possible, while in the process of listing potential problems, look for an alteration to the plan that will completely sidestep a potential problem without impacting the success of the strategy.

Assess Impact and Probability

Look at the likely impact of each potential problem and ask the team to consider whether the impact of that problem will be high, medium, or low. Then assess the probability that each threat will occur and mark this high, medium, and low as well. As your team members implement the strategy and begin to think long term, they will start to spend more time on high probability rather than low impact threats. The most significant threats are those with the greatest potential impact and a high probability of occurrence.

Minimize Risks

When you have assessed which risks are likely to threaten the viability of the project formulate a contingency plan to mitigate their effects.

```
Brainstorm
   ⇩
Consider the threat
   ⇩
Mark each threat
   ⇩
Formulate a contingency plan
```

Are You in Control of Potential Threats?

Successful teams will minimize the amount of time they spend on low probability threats and concentrate on the high urgency ones that threaten the continuing viability of the change project they are working on.

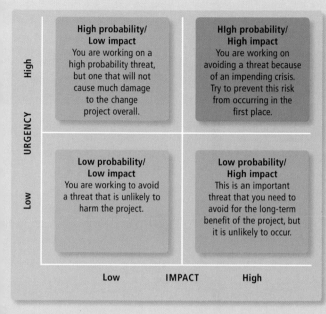

Use this matrix to assess the urgency of any risks that might threaten the success of the project.

→ Ask yourself—in which of these boxes do I mainly work?
→ High impact risks that have a high probability of occurring are the most pressing and should always be dealt with as a matter of urgency.
→ Low impact risks, or those that have a low probability of occurring, are not so urgent.

Summary: Actioning the Plan

Set the priorities for the team from those needs of the organization that have been identified as urgent and make the necessary changes to the plan to deliver solutions to problems. Look at the risks involved and then just go ahead and do it. Figure out how to motivate and encourage your team to achieve its goals.

Getting Ready for Change

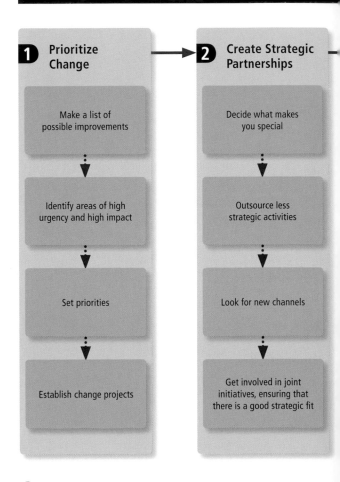

1 Prioritize Change

Make a list of possible improvements

Identify areas of high urgency and high impact

Set priorities

Establish change projects

2 Create Strategic Partnerships

Decide what makes you special

Outsource less strategic activities

Look for new channels

Get involved in joint initiatives, ensuring that there is a good strategic fit

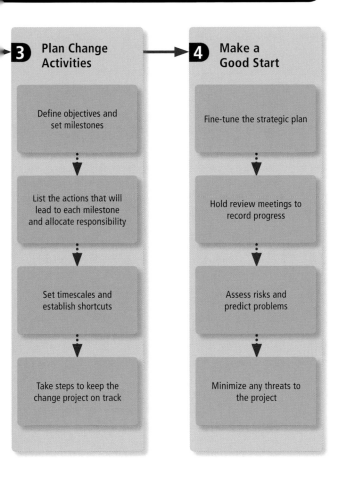

3 Plan Change Activities

→ **4** Make a Good Start

Define objectives and set milestones

⋮

List the actions that will lead to each milestone and allocate responsibility

⋮

Set timescales and establish shortcuts

⋮

Take steps to keep the change project on track

Fine-tune the strategic plan

⋮

Hold review meetings to record progress

⋮

Assess risks and predict problems

⋮

Minimize any threats to the project

Review Goals

A new strategy means that there will be some changes in emphasis and some improvements to the working environment. Agree on new targets for the performance of the team and that of each team member individually.

Reset Targets

Break down the top-level objectives of the strategy, divide them into specific measurable targets at the next level, and so on down the team to the individual members. Make the targets achievable, but keep them realistic as well. Once individual targets have been agreed upon, check that each member of the team has the skills required to achieve success. If not, look for ways of developing those skills in a time- and cost-effective way.

think SMART

Most team members could perform better if they had more resources of people or money. Use the offer of a new target to increase your resources so that you can exploit new opportunities.

Explain to your manager what your strategy is, pointing out the increased opportunities. Offer to accept a higher target if you are given more resources. Your manager will probably jump at the chance to improve performance so you need to make it absolutely clear that it is not an option to accept the new target without the additional resources. When you have received a commitment to the resources you need, you can draw up a new strategic plan.

> **Companies should measure their success by how many opportunities they have missed.**
>
> Gary Hemel

Make Further Improvements

As the team achieves its new targets, the strategy will develop and make it possible for you to look for more areas that could improve effectiveness, efficiency, or customer service. Most organizations compete in markets where customer expectations are constantly increasing and competitors are improving their ability to satisfy them. Ensure that your internal targets keep in step with the changing needs and increasing competition. For example, you may have reduced costs as compared to last year, but can you keep them at that level and still improve quality and service? It is not logical to wait for the start of a new company year to reset your targets. Review them continuously and encourage people to suggest how they can improve productivity.

Explain to the team how strategic thinking can benefit performance today as well as in the future. When you are developing the strategy it is important to ensure that team members are committed to their new targets and feel confident in their ability to achieve them.

Improve Performance and Results

Start the implementation of the new strategy

⬇

Implement the change projects

⬇

Review operational targets

⬇

Produce an operating plan for the team with the new targets

⬇

Ask team members to create their own plans for operational tasks and personal development

⬇

Achieve improved performance and results

Define Your Dashboard

To monitor your performance against the strategy you need to have a mental picture of a control panel that resembles a car's dashboard—indicators and warning lights will tell you how good your performance is.

Establish Key Performance Indicators

All teams and organizations need information about past performance and indications of trends for the future. These indicators are known as KPIs (Key Performance Indicators) and provide an effective mechanism for confirming whether your strategy is correct. There may be many possible indicators to choose from. Think carefully about the targets that your organization sets you and choose no more than three to six indicators that will clearly tell you where there is any danger that you are not going

Aim for a Balanced Scorecard

While financial KPIs are very important, they are not the only type of indicator that you need. Kaplan and Norton, the inventors of the term "balanced scorecard," advise team leaders to look for indicators in four areas:

→ **Financial results**—Are we hitting our financial targets (income, revenues, operating costs, profitability)?
→ **Customer and brand**—How are we viewed by our customers and the market?
→ **Operations and process**—Are our current business processes efficient and effective?
→ **Learning and growth**—How can we continue to learn, improve, add value, and develop our skills?

Work out appropriate KPIs in these four areas for your team.

Avoid Performance Failure

HIGH IMPACT

- Using green, amber, and red symbols with key indicators to show if everything is on track, if there is a danger of a problem occurring, or if a problem has occurred already
- Reviewing KPIs regularly, particularly when something important has changed that might affect the plan
- Using KPIs to show potential areas of concern

NEGATIVE IMPACT

- Making KPIs too complex, so that people find them difficult to understand
- Hoping that the KPIs set at the beginning of the year will still be appropriate at the end of the year and failing to review them
- Using KPIs only to tell you when something has gone wrong
- Failing to take action when your KPIs reveal that your performance is lacking

---

to hit your strategic goals. Now think about it from the customer's point of view and establish three to six indicators that will show that you are going to provide a high level of customer satisfaction both now and in the future. Be careful that you're not overachieving in one area at the expense of another, leading to dissatisfied customers. KPIs are also an effective bridge between a team member's job and strategic achievement. The team members may not all need to know and understand the whole strategic plan, but if they are achieving success with their specific key indicators, then they are playing their part in the successful implementation of the strategy.

Flashing warning lights always indicate a problem

TIP Even if there is no environmental regulation in your industry, it is a good idea to identify KPIs that show how environmentally friendly your operation is.

Choose a Leadership Style

Choose an appropriate leadership style for each team and for individual team members. Remember that the best leadership style in a crisis is unlikely to be the same as one that is appropriate to a steady-state operation.

Involve Others

If you have used team-planning sessions as your way of creating your strategic plan, you have already made a start on an involvement style of management. You have consulted with people, listened to their views, and agreed to a way ahead by consensus. Be aware, however, that leadership of a project team, particularly a change project team, means operating with a spectrum of styles, from simply directing someone to perform a task, to working on group discussion and consensus. Ensure that each team member understands his role within the whole strategy.

Adapt to the Individual

A famous sports figure was said to have "a degree in people." When people analyzed how he operated it came down mainly to knowing his people really well and how to lead each individual.

→ **Objective oriented people** just want to be told what their objective is, what resources they will have, and when their part is to be completed. They enjoy figuring out how to achieve objectives and will only refer to you for regular review and for help if they encounter a snag. Don't tell these people how to do their job; they love to figure it out for themselves.

→ **Task oriented people** are not comfortable about accepting their part in a project without agreeing on the detailed steps and actions that they will have to perform to achieve the objective. Don't put them in situations where they might feel directionless and uncertain about what to do.

Delegate Effectively

Think creatively by deciding which tasks you can delegate to other members of the team. Hand over tasks and then help the team to match or exceed the

Be Inclusive The team leader should not be involved in the day-to-day tasks of the project. Make sure that you delegate to the right people so that you can lead the team as the project moves forward as planned.

quality of work you expect. Interfering, countermanding instructions and decisions made by the delegated person, and oversupervision are all very bad for morale and are signs of poor leadership. Remember that delegating is not only about getting tasks done and achieving objectives; it is also about managing your time and developing the skills and capabilities of team members. Supervise performance with occasional face-to-face meetings and regular reports. Observe how well people are working and developing.

TIP Leadership is about getting people to give of their best. Find out how to inspire and motivate each individual member of the team.

Motivate People

Motivate everyone involved in your strategy by ensuring that they understand their role. Encourage them to succeed by offering them appropriate training and rewarding their efforts and achievements.

Show Appreciation

Expressing your appreciation of people's efforts is vital if you are to get the best out of them. Check that the old reward system fits the new environment. If you have changed targets, roles, and responsibilities, you may have to offer new reward and incentives. Remember that mentoring and coaching are an essential part of an environment where you are continuously trying to improve performance and service to customers. Give your team the support it needs to do the job

Efforts and achievements should be rewarded

well, and do not forget about other stakeholders—they need your help and appreciation in performing their roles. Give feedback when things have gone well.

Motivate Your Team

HIGH IMPACT

- Encouraging suggestions from the team on ways to change and improve performance
- Making roles and responsibilities clear to everyone involved
- Assuming that people want to achieve more
- Asking stakeholders to meet the team informally to demonstrate their interest

NEGATIVE IMPACT

- Being inflexible about changing the original plan
- Leaving doubt as to who is responsible for what
- Assuming that people are lazy and do not like working
- Making the project team appear to others as a clique
- Keeping a distance between the team and the stakeholders

Encourage Teamwork

A team is worth much more than the sum of the individual members. Being proud of being a member of a particular team is highly motivational. Encourage people by giving them complete tasks that they can take from start to finish and allow them to decide on the best way of working. In this way you are enabling them to use their talents more fully. Encourage everyone involved to make a contribution to the matter at hand. Set aside time to talk to each team member to discuss that individual's tasks, ideas, and feelings about progress. Show, in meetings, how people are contributing to the team's performance and encourage them to promote teamwork when talking to colleagues. Allow individuals and teams to show how good they are. When people feel that their contribution is appreciated they will perform better.

Choose the Right Type of Training Intervention By changing their roles and responsibilities, you may find that previously well-qualified members of the team now lack the skills to achieve their new targets. List the skills your people need for their current and future roles and plan the correct type of training intervention to fill any gaps.

Training Intervention
- Formal interventions
- Informal interventions
- Conferences
- Visits
- Training courses
- Self-study
- Accredited qualifications
- Briefing sessions
- On-the job mentoring
- Team reflection and brainstorming
- Coaching assignments
- Supervision

Hold Reviews

Review meetings allow you to check if you are achieving your new operational targets. They can also be used to monitor how the change projects are going and if they are on track in terms of time and budget.

Review Progress

Your team should hold monthly review meetings. Use the status indicators—red, amber, or green—to establish the order of the agenda of the meeting. Monitor the previous month's operational performance to see how you have done. Look at change projects and assess whether you are actually making the changes in the way that you intended. The discussion on these points will lead to a number of suggestions for changing the way you work. Finally, check whether your plan is still valid in all aspects.

Keep to the Point

Many teams find that discussion of operating issues takes up a lot of time at review meetings. This means that discussion of long-term strategy can get sidelined. Do not let this happen or your strategic plan will stagnate and lose its relevance and credibility.

TECHNIQUES *to* practice

Try to set aside some time at the monthly meetings to review the overall strategy.

- Check the assumptions you identified at fact-gathering stage to confirm that they still hold true.
- Regroup products if there has been innovation or change.
- Change the emphasis on product/markets.
- Reexamine budgets to see if you still have the resources to complete the plan and look for more if you don't.
- Spend time looking ahead and proactively identifying and mitigating risks.

Resolve Issues

Discuss indicators that show when immediate action is required; they are probably marked status red. For example, if a change in emphasis has gone well and you are selling more to a particular product/market, you may run into delivery problems. Get the team to decide what to do about it, agree who is responsible for resolving the issue, and put a time limit on finding a solution. Put the obvious person in charge. If a point comes up regularly and shows no improvement, check what action actually is feasible and change the plan rather than leaving the problem to fester. However, if just two people are involved in an issue, do not take up the time of the whole team in an attempt to find a solution to the problem—assign those two people to discuss it subsequently.

> **The greatest challenge to any thinker is stating the problem in a way that will allow a solution.**
>
> Bertrand Russell

Be Flexible

An army general once said, "No plan survives contact with the enemy." No strategic plan survives contact with the marketplace. Be prepared to change the plan in the light of new circumstances and the unforeseen.

Expect the Unexpected

It is not possible to predict every possibility that might occur during the implementation of your plan. External events, such as a change in regulation, may force you to review a basic item in the plan when it is only a short time into implementation. A radical change, such as a competitive product announcement or the merging of two large customers, may require extensive changes to the original plan. Whenever such a change happens, and certainly every year, make sure that you reexamine the plan from the starting point, the overall statement of direction, all the way to the end.

Retest the Strategy

The strategy at the end of the planning year may look different from your initial plan, but it should still reflect the best speed and direction of development. The benefit of using the business plan template will occur again when the team makes changes to the strategy.

→ Subject each change, such as a change of emphasis on a product/market, to the business case template by checking how well it rates against each of your key criterion. This will reveal more clearly which opportunities you should exploit.

→ Although there will be times when you have to review even the business case template, you should come to realize that this is what strategic thinking is all about: keeping up to date and improving all the time.

Case study: Adapting to Change

Adam was about to sign a contract with a contractor to build a new pumping station to serve 200 new houses being served by the water company, for which he was a project manager. Joe, his team leader, insisted that Adam talk to the planning commission and check that his part of the strategy for water distribution was still relevant. At the meeting with the planners it was revealed that the same developer had made a planning application for another 100 houses. Adam delayed the original plan and the team reviewed the strategy, changing the size and timing of the pumping system.

- *By insisting that Adam speak to the planning commission again, Joe made sure that the team did not pursue a strategy that might have necessitated two pumping projects rather than one, significantly increasing the cost.*
- *By having in place a strategic plan that was in the end a framework, the team was able to adapt to the new situation.*

Alter Course

Be prepared to change the strategic plan as and when necessary. One of the benefits of a good strategic plan is that, even in fast-moving business circumstances, the strategy provides the basis on which to evaluate opportunities. To remain effective you and your team must constantly challenge your current methods of doing business and seek to change and improve the ways in which you meet customer needs. A difficult situation arises, for example, if a competitor offering something radically better has made an important project for a new product irrelevant. Just as your reviewing system must allow the exploitation of new opportunities, it must also provide a mechanism for discarding originally sound ideas. Altering the course may also require additional resources.

While the strategic plan may change, the framework will remain in place

Set a Life Strategy 5

Ambitious people sometimes find themselves working so hard that they lose out in the nonworking part of their lives. It is vital that you make a decision about your work/life balance and plan how you are going to use your time. This chapter will help you to:

- Plan a strategy for your working and nonworking life
- Plan your work/life balance
- Help yourself and others to think about their lives, both working and nonworking
- Plan how you want your career to progress

Plan a Life Strategy

As important as your work strategy is to you, your team, and your organization, it is not as important as setting a wider strategy for your life. Consider how much time you will put into work, and what else you want to do.

Be at One with Yourself

When you were a child you obeyed your parents. Even when you rebelled against their values in your teens, you were still not necessarily being your own person. That comes later. You come to realize that being happy is not only important in itself, but a crucial ingredient in your success, both at work and in life.

Your life can be as successful as you want it to be

What Do You Want?

Just as in your team strategy you laid down clear objectives, so in your everyday life be sure what you mean by success, not only at work but also with regard to your other aspirations to succeed in relationships and in your growth as a person. Ask yourself:

- What kind of relationship do I want to have with my spouse or partner in life?
- What sort of parent do I want to be?
- What are the values that I want my children to have as they grow up?

Take time to think about these matters on a regular basis, and form a strategic plan for where you want to be and by when. If you sometimes feel that your life is without direction it may be simply because you haven't taken the time to decide what you want from it.

We judge ourselves by what we think we are capable of. Others judge us by what we have done.

Henry Longfellow

Find a Balance

There are 168 hours in the week, of which you spend up to 68 in bed, leaving 100 waking hours. Draw a three by three matrix of nine boxes and in each box write an activity heading from the list of suggested activities below.

→ friends	→ health
→ relationships	→ hobbies
→ family	→ leisure
→ time alone	→ creativity
→ personal development	→ work

Use the grid to create more time for yourself and get your work/ life balance right. Count the number of hours you spend in each of these areas every week, and write this figure as a percentage (12 hours = 12%) in the appropriate box. Look at any areas where you would like to make adjustments, but remember that for every area whose percentage you increase you will have to decrease the percentage of time allocated to another area. When you have finished, see if you can achieve a balance by reallocating some time to more fulfilling activities.

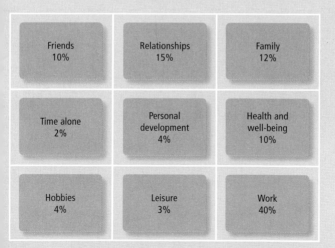

Friends 10%	Relationships 15%	Family 12%
Time alone 2%	Personal development 4%	Health and well-being 10%
Hobbies 4%	Leisure 3%	Work 40%

Be a Sounding Board

HIGH IMPACT

- Giving your undivided attention to someone who is speaking
- Articulating ideas to remove any loose ends or cloudy thinking
- Relying on your gut feeling as well as logical thought when making decisions

NEGATIVE IMPACT

- Plainly working out what you are going to say next when someone else is speaking
- Expecting silent thought to lead to the best decision
- Deciding to do something that feels instinctively wrong for you

Maintain a Flexible Approach

There was a time when people could plan to work for the same organization all their working lives. For most people that time has long gone, and we can expect to work for several organizations during our careers. Your life strategy should therefore be much broader than envisioning success within the organization where you currently work. You should be prepared to move to another job if an opportunity arises in another organization that makes your success and long-term-happiness more likely.

TECHNIQUES
to practice

A good way of achieving happiness and success in the future is to practice a visualization.
Set aside an hour to be alone and find a quiet place to sit down with a pen and some paper. Now imagine the best six months of your life—a six-month period that you might dream about.

- Picture yourself, aged 95, telling your great grandchildren about this six months, how happy you are, what a great job you are in, what relationships you are enjoying, and so on.
- Write this down in detail.
- Put it somewhere that you can see it every day, and read it each morning.

Facilitate Good Decisions

The quality of our decisions is governed to some extent by the sort of thinking that precedes it. Practice active thinking by getting together with friends or colleagues and acting as a sounding board for each other's thoughts and concerns.

Environment Busy environments can affect the quality of the decisions that we make. Find somewhere that is conducive to relaxation and helps you to take time out to think and share information.

Discussion Sit down with a friend and encourage her to explain her thoughts and concerns. Try not to offer any advice, but simply act as a sounding board for her thinking.

Listening Use nods and encouraging words to show that you're paying attention but try not to offer too many opinions. This will help her to come to decisions herself. Now ask her to do the same for you.

Make Choices

Develop a positive mental attitude to achieving the vision that you have for your life. Such an attitude transforms a glass from being half empty to being half full, and then it can actually help to fill the glass. Everything you do is your choice. Suppose, for example, that you have to attend a meeting every month that you feel serves no purpose. You go because the team leader insists that you do.

- Remember that, despite the pressure from above, it is still your choice to go to the meeting.
- Having a positive mental attitude means looking on the meeting as an opportunity to meet colleagues, to get to know them better, and, most importantly, to add as much value to the meeting as you can.
- Make suggestions and offer your contribution. You may find that the usefulness of the meeting improves.
- Take the same positive attitude toward activities that you regard as chores in your daily life.

Case study: Getting to Know Yourself

When Gladys was first married she did everything for her husband. She cooked, she cleaned, she washed and ironed, put out his clothes, and run all the household errands. When she became a mother she found it impossible to continue to look after her husband in the same way and felt guilty about it. And, now she felt guilt about her performance as a mother as well. Her friend Ann took her aside and asked her, "Who is the real Gladys?" That question made her think about who she was and who she wanted to be. She began to visualize her future life, defined what for her was success, and changed how she behaved to live up to her own expectations rather than the expectations that she perceived others had of her.

• By making Gladys think about success and her own values, Ann had opened the door to a new Gladys, one who could be successful on her own terms.
• Ann had shown her that what she had been trying to achieve was impossible and causing her to feel guilty and unhappy.

think
SMART

Harness the power of positive thinking, and even those tasks you most dreaded having to do will begin to seem more manageable.

Imagine that you have completed a task you don't want to do. Think how good you will feel about getting the task done. Set aside some time to do it, remembering that it is your choice whether you approach it feeling depressed or energized. If you feel depressed the task will become more of a chore and the quality of thinking you put into it will be reduced.

Take Charge of Your Life

Do not let anyone take your life visions away from you. It is usually the people closest to you who will divert you from your dream—a father, for example, may try to persuade a daughter to aim for a more stable career than being a musician, despite the fact that she has wanted to become a musician since she was very young. The father is doing it because he wants his daughter to take fewer risks of being frustrated or unhappy; but the truth is he is stealing her dream. Take control and be proactive at all times. When things go wrong do not take the victim's approach of blaming other people; but ask yourself what you could have done to make the outcome different. Accept that things, even in the best-planned lives, do go wrong for reasons outside your control—that's life, move on.

5 minute FIX

For a quick change to your work/life balance do not try to analyze all your waking time.

- Take the two key areas where you want to spend more time. and the two key areas on which you feel you spend too much time.
- Work out a way of changing the balance.

Summary: Setting a Life Strategy

If you recognize the need for a good strategic plan at work, you must also recognize how important it is to fit your part in that into how you live. Think about your long-term career as well as the success of your organization. Get your work/life balance right and remember that the strategy is to have fun as well as make a living.

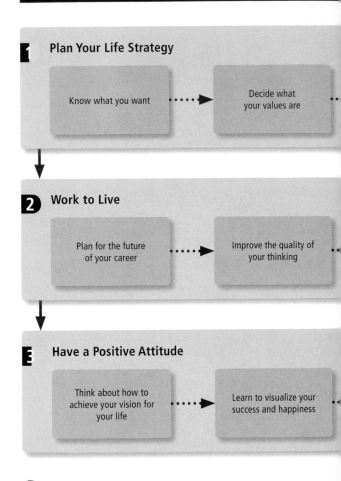

Finding a Balance

1 **Plan Your Life Strategy**

Know what you want ·····▶ Decide what your values are ··

2 **Work to Live**

Plan for the future of your career ·····▶ Improve the quality of your thinking ··

3 **Have a Positive Attitude**

Think about how to achieve your vision for your life ·····▶ Learn to visualize your success and happiness

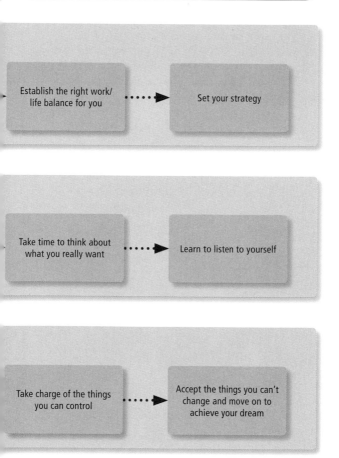

Establish the right work/life balance for you ......➤ Set your strategy

Take time to think about what you really want ......➤ Learn to listen to yourself

Take charge of the things you can control ......➤ Accept the things you can't change and move on to achieve your dream

Plan a Career Strategy

In conjunction with your life and business strategies,
think about your career strategy. Extend the possibilities
by developing a network of contacts and use the annual
review to get agreement on what you want to do.

Extend Your Contacts

Success in life will often come down to the people you
know and work with or choose to spend time with. Avoid
losing contact details by keeping a lifetime address book,
preferably electronically. Never assume that a person who
has had just a passing influence on your career will never
be in a position to be helpful to you again. You will find
that your groups of business and personal contacts will
often be the source of future career changes or personal
challenges. Salespeople knows this better than anyone.
They keep the name and number of every contact they
make throughout their working lives. Think about this
potential network of opportunity in career terms and build
your contacts high and wide in your organization.

Make the Most of Opportunities

VOLUNTEER FOR TASKS	Get exposure to senior managers
ACCEPT TRANSFERS	Extend your knowledge and experience
USE CHANCE MEETINGS	Use every chance meeting as an opportunity for advancement
KEEP DETAILS	Keep all contact names; every name can be useful

Take Responsibility

The annual review is vital to your career plan and an excellent
example of the importance of taking responsibility for your own
career. Reviews form a continuous record of your achievements
and developments over time, so take them seriously. Ask yourself:

→ What value have you added in your job?
→ Where is it that you would like to go?
→ What do you need to get there?
→ Why should your manager support these plans?
→ What is the benefit to the organization?

Answering these questions will help you to make the most
productive use of this opportunity. Take ownership of your career
and impress your manager with your motivation and your obvious
determination. Having a clear idea of your career strategy is much
more impressive than accepting whatever is suggested without
having any proposals of your own.

• Volunteer for tasks that give you exposure to senior
  managers. The company newsletter or the annual
  conference are good examples of this.
• Accept temporary transfers to staff projects. Think
  broadly about this—is there another organization that
  you could work for on a temporary basis that would
  extend your network and experience?
• Always know what you would say to a high-level person
  that you meet by chance, in the elevator, for example.
  High-level people are open to new ideas from any source,
  even someone relatively new to the company.

TIP Accept any opportunity for training. However
distant the skills taught are from those required by
your current role, they may be useful in your next one.

Index

Picture Credits

The publisher would like to thank the following for their kind permission to reproduce their photographs: Abbreviations key : (l) = left, (c) = center, (r) = right, (t) = top, (b) = below, (cl) = center left, (cr) = center right.

1: LWA/The Image Bank/Getty (l), Altrendo Images/Getty (c), Tony Mataxas/Asia Images/Getty (r); **2:** Tony Anderson/Iconica/Getty; **3:** LWA- JDC/Corbis (t), Michael Hemsley (c), William Edward King/Iconica/Getty (b); **5:** David Gould/Photographer's Choice/Getty; **7:** Jose Luis Pelaez, Inc./Corbis; **8:** David Trood/Stone+/Getty (l), Michael Hemsley (cl), Johner Images/Getty (cr), Andreas Pollok/Taxi/Getty (r); **13:** Michael Hemsley; **15:** Michael Hemsley; **17:** Michael Hemsley; **18:** LWA-JDC/Corbis; **23:** Ryanstock/Taxi/Getty; **25:** Michael Hemsley; **30:** White Packert/Photonica/Getty; **43:** Wide Group/Iconica/Getty; **45:** Johner Images/Getty; **47:** Tony Mataxas/Asia Images/Getty; **49:** David Gould/Photographer's Choice/Getty; **50:** Andreas Pollok/Taxi/Getty; **57:** Ausloeser/zefa/Corbis; **62:** Ingo Boddenberg/zefa/Corbis; **65:** Andreas Pollok/Taxi/Getty; **75:** Michael Hemsley; **80:** Altrendo Images/Getty; **85:** LWA/The Image Bank/Getty; **86:** David Trood/Stone+/Getty; **89:** Wide Group/Iconica/Getty; **93:** LWA/The Image Bank/Getty; **99:** William Edward King/Iconica/Getty; **107:** Michael Hemsley; **111:** Martin Riedl/Taxi/Getty; **115:** IT Int'l/Jupiter Images.

All other images © Dorling Kindersley.

For further information see www.dkimages.com

Authors' acknowledgments

Writing a book for Dorling Kindersley is a most interesting exercise in teamwork. We would like to thank Adèle Hayward and Simon Tuite for their stewardship of the design and the process. Thank you also to the editor, Fiona Biggs, for her constructive feedback and huge contribution to improving the script. Finally, thank you all for making it such an enjoyable task.

Authors' biographies

Andy Bruce is founder and Chief Executive of SofTools—a UK-based business solutions company (www.SofTools.net). Over the last 15 years he has worked with clients in both the public and private sectors to enable senior management visibility and control, and sustained performance improvement. He is also an affiliate lecturer at Henley Management College.

Ken Langdon has a background in sales and marketing in the technology industry. As an independent consultant he has trained salespeople and sales managers in the US, Europe, and Australia, and has advised managers on the coaching and review of their staff. He has also provided strategic guidance for companies including computer major Hewlett Packard. Ken is the author of a number of books for DK and co-author of several Essential Managers titles, including *Putting Customers First*. He is also one of the authors of DK's *Successful Manager's Handbook*.